Ottawa – Hull

2nd edition

Pascale Couture

Travel better, enjoy more

ULYSSES

Travel Guides

Offices

CANADA: Ulysses Travel Guides, 4176 Saint-Denis, Montréal, Québec, H2W 2M5, ☎ (514) 843-9447 or 1-877-542-7247, ⌗(514) 843-9448, info@ulysses.ca, www.ulyssesguides.com

EUROPE: Les Guides de Voyage Ulysse SARL, BP 159, 75523 Paris Cedex 11, France, ☎ 01 43 38 89 50, ⌗01 43 38 89 52, voyage@ulysse.ca, www.ulyssesguides.com

U.S.A.: Ulysses Travel Guides, 305 Madison Avenue, Suite 1166, New York, NY 10165, ☎ 1-877-542-7247, info@ulysses.ca, www.ulyssesguides.com

Distributors

CANADA: Ulysses Books & Maps, 4176 Saint-Denis, Montréal, Québec, H2W 2M5, ☎ (514) 843-9882, ext.2232, 800-748-9171, Fax: 514-843-9448, info@ulysses.ca, www.ulyssesguides.com

GREAT BRITAIN AND IRELAND: World Leisure Marketing, Unit 11, Newmarket Court, Newmarket Drive, Derby DE24 8NW, ☎ 1 332 57 37 37, Fax: 1 332 57 33 99, office@wlmsales.co.uk

SCANDINAVIA: Scanvik, Esplanaden 8B, 1263 Copenhagen K, DK, ☎ (45) 33.12.77.66, Fax: (45) 33.91.28.82

SPAIN: Altaïr, Balmes 69, E-08007 Barcelona, ☎ 454 29 66, Fax: 451 25 59, altair@globalcom.es

SWITZERLAND: OLF, P.O. Box 1061, CH-1701 Fribourg, ☎ (026) 467.51.11, Fax: (026) 467.54.66

U.S.A.: The Globe Pequot Press, 246 Goose Lane, Guilford, CT 06437 - 0480, ☎1-800-243-0495, Fax: 800-820-2329, sales@globe-pequot.com

Other countries contact Ulysses Books & Maps, 4176 Saint-Denis, Montréal, Québec, H2W 2M5, ☎ (514) 843-9882, ext.2232, ☎ 800-748-9171, Fax: 514-843-9448, info@ulysses.ca, www.ulyssesguides.com

Canadian Cataloguing-in-Publication Data (see page 4)
© March 2001, Ulysses Travel Guides.
All rights reserved. Printed in Canada
ISBN 2-89464-331-4

Grandeur is written on thy throne,
Beauty encompasseth thy mien;
The glory of the North alone,
Is thine, O Ottawa, my Queen.

James E. Caldwell
"Ottawa," 1907

Author
Pascale Couture

Editor
Pascale Couture

Publisher
Pascale Couture

Project Coordinator
Jacqueline Grekin

Copy Editing
Eileen Connolly
Anne Joyce

Translation
Christina Poole
Cindy Garayt
Tracey Kendrick
Danielle Gauthier
Sarah Kresh

Page Layout
Anne Joyce

Cartographers
André Duchesne
Bradley Fenton
Patrick Thivierge
Yanik Landreville

Computer Graphics
Stéphanie Routhier

Artistic Director
Patrick Farei (Atoll)

Illustrations
Lorette Pierson
Jenny Jasper

Photography
Cover page
Grant V. Faint/
The Image Bank
Inside pages
P. Quittemelle/
Megapress
Neil Valois/Megapress
Tibor Bognár

Thanks to: Benoît Prieur, François Hénault, Alana Engler and Claude Morneau.

We acknowledge the financial support of the Government of Canada through the Book Publishing Industry Development Program (BPIDP) for our publishing activities.

We would also like to thank SODEC (Québec) for its financial support.

Canadian Cataloguing-in-Publication Data

Couture, Pascale, 1966-

Ottawa-Hull

(Ulysses travel guide)
Includes index.

ISBN 2-89464-331-4

1. National Capital Region (Ont. and Québec) - Guidebooks. 2. Ottawa Metropolitan Area (Ont.) - Guidebooks. 3. Hull Region (Québec) - Guidebooks. I. Title. II. Series.

FC2783.C68 2001   917.13'83044   C2001-940011-X
F1054.O9C68 2001

Table of Contents

List of Maps

Map Symbols

?	Tourist information (permanent service)	🏛	Museum
?	Tourist information (Seasonal service)	🛄	Train station
⊛	National capital	✈	Airport
✪	Provincial capital	-----	Bike path

Symbols

bkfst incl.	Breakfast included
≈	Fax number
⊖	Fitness centre
K	Kitchenette
pb	Private bathroom
≋	Pool
ℜ	Restaurant
△	Sauna
sb	Shared bathroom
☎	Telephone number
⊛	Whirlpool
	Ulysses's favourite
♿	Wheelchair access

ATTRACTION CLASSIFICATION

★	Interesting
★★	Worth a visit
★★★	Not to be missed

HOTEL CLASSIFICATION

Unless otherwise indicated, the prices in the guide are for one standard room, double occupancy in high season.

RESTAURANT CLASSIFICATION

$	$10 or less
$$	$10 to $20
$$$	$20 to $30
$$$$	$30 or more

The prices in the guide are for a meal for one person, not including drinks and tip.

All prices in this guide are in Canadian dollars.

Write to Us

The information contained in this guide was correct at press time. However, mistakes can slip in, omissions are always possible, places can disappear, etc. The authors and publisher hereby disclaim any liability for loss or damage resulting from omissions or errors.

We value your comments, corrections and suggestions, as they allow us to keep each guide up to date. The best contributions will be rewarded with a free book from Ulysses Travel Guides. All you have to do is write us at the following address and indicate which title you would be interested in receiving (see the list at the end of the guide).

Ulysses Travel Guides
4176 Saint-Denis
Montréal, Québec
Canada H2W 2M5
www.ulyssesguides.com
E-mail: text@ulysses.ca

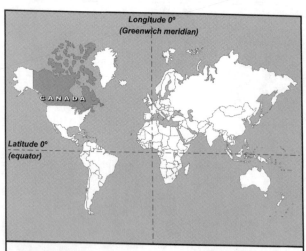

Longitude 0°
(Greenwich meridian)

CANADA

Latitude 0°
(equator)

 Where are Ottawa and Hull ?

©ULYSSES

CANADA
Capital: Ottawa
Population: 30,300,000 inhab.
Currency: Canadian dollar
Area: 9,970,610 km²

ONTARIO
Capital: Toronto
Population: 10,753,573 inhab.
Area: 1,068,630 km²

N

YUKON
N.W.T.
NUNAVUT
NEWFOUNDLAND
BRITISH COLUMBIA
ALBERTA
SASKATCHEWAN
MANITOBA
Hudson Bay
QUÉBEC
ONTARIO
P.E.I.
N.B.
N.S.
Ottawa
Hull
Pacific Ocean
Atlantic Ocean

UNITED STATES

Portrait

Europearopean explorers were first drawn to this area because of its location on the banks of the Ottawa River near the Chaudière Falls.

Later, this site, covered by a seemingly infinite forest, was deemed strategic to British authorities, who decided to dig a canal and build a village here. In less than 200 years, this tiny hamlet metamorphosed into a dynamic city which is now Canada's national capital. Strolling along its streets, you can see for yourself just how lovely a city Ottawa has become, with its splendid Victorian buildings, vast green spaces and outstanding museums that boast some of the finest collections in the country.

Geography

When Europeans began exploring Canada, the Ottawa River immediately became one of the major access routes into the new territory. It was not, however, the easiest route, for it was studded with all sorts of natural obstacles, including the Chaudière Falls. It was at the foot of these falls that two towns sprouted up—first Wrightown (Hull), on the north shore, then Bytown (Ottawa), on the south shore, at the mouth of the Rideau River. Ottawa is therefore on the Ontario side of the Ottawa

(Outaouais) River, while Hull is on the Québec side.

These two towns were set in the midst of a dense forest comprised of a variety of vegetation, with evergreens such as pine, spruce and fir, as well as a smaller number of deciduous species, such as aspen, birch and willow. The acidity of the soil made the land ill-suited to farming, so early settlers gradually gave up on agriculture and turned to the forest for their livelihood. Over the years, the lumber industry flourished, causing the forest to shrink dramatically. Fortunately, the creation of Gatineau National Park (Québec) has allowed, a vast expanse of woodland has survived untouched.

Population

Ottawa evolved from a tiny village in the heart of a dense forest to a proud and beautiful capital city within the space of a century. Today, Ottawa and its region (including the cities of Hull, Kanata, Vanier, Aylmer and Gatineau) are home to more than a million inhabitants. The population of Ottawa has an English-speaking majority (51%), but it also has a large French-speaking population, particularly on the Québec side (33%). It also

The Odawa

Ottawa was named after the Algonquian tribe that used to live in the Ottawa Valley. The name apparently means "to trade." These First Nations people lived on farming, hunting, fishing and trade, and used the Ottawa River as a route inland. Their economy, closely linked to those of other tribes such as the Huron, who lived on the shores of Georgian Bay, was greatly disrupted by the arrival of the first Europeans. When the Iroquois destroyed Huronia in 1649, the Odawa were forced to flee westward. They didn't return to Ontario until about 20 years later, when they settled on Manitoulin Island and around the Great Lakes.

includes people whose mother tongue is another language (15%), notably Arabic, Chinese and Italian.

History

Ottawa did not spring into being spontaneously. In fact, it was founded fairly late (1825) in response to military and political imperatives, unlike older cities such as Montréal and New York, which were born principally of commerce. Ottawa owes its existence to the events that took place when Europeans first started colonizing Canada. Hull, on the other hand, was founded some 25 years earlier when a small community headed by Phileman Wright was set up on the opposite shore of the Ottawa River, creating Wrightstown.

Colonization

Officially, John Cabot became the first European to reach the shores of Canada, in 1497. He was followed by Jacques Cartier, who first arrived in 1534 then subsequently returned on two other voyages. In search of a route to Asia, Cartier sailed along the coast of Labrador and up the St. Lawrence River to a native settlement named Hochelaga, located on the site now occupied by Montréal. There was no real follow-up to these voyages, however. In fact, it wasn't until the early 17th century that France started taking an interest in Canada once again, due to the demand for fur clothing in Europe. Little by little, permanent trading posts were established on the Atlantic coast and inland in order to strengthen ties with native suppliers. In 1605, Port-Royal, in Acadia, was built; then, in 1608, Champlain and his men founded Québec City, which started out as a handful of fortified buildings. A permanent French presence was thus established in North America.

In the early years of colonization, French activity in North America centred mainly around the fur trade, as well as the efforts of missionaries, who were determined to convert the natives to Christianity. The French didn't develop the Ottawa region. However, they knew it well since the

Ottawa River was then an important navigational route, allowing explorers to discover new territory. At the same time, the French slowly began to populate the territory. In 1663, when New France became a French province, it only had 3,000 inhabitants.

New France reached its apogee at the dawn of the 18th century, when it had a monopoly on the fur trade in North America and controlled the St. Lawrence River. However, in 1713, after being defeated in Europe, the French handed over control of Hudson's Bay and Acadia to the English, who thus obtained part of the fur trade and a number of strategic military posts. In 1763, four years after Québec City was conquered by the British, France ceded New France to England under the Treaty of Paris. At the time, the territory was inhabited by some 60,000 French colonists.

In the years following the British Conquest, the Canadian population was still largely French. The territory west of the Ottawa River remained virtually unsettled, occupied only by native bands and fur traders. At that time, the British Crown had no plans to colonize or develop the territory beyond expanding the fur trade.

The American Revolution (1775-1783), however, led to the founding of Ontario and radically changed the history of Canada. In the first few years of this war between Great Britain and her 13 colonies in southern North America, British troops scouted out strategic positions in Ontario from which to launch attacks on the American rebels. Overall, however, the British and their allies found themselves at a disadvantage, and finally had to accept defeat. The American Revolution, at least in the beginning, was a true civil war pitting supporters of American independence against Loyalists wishing to maintain colonial ties with Great Britain. Over 350,000 of the latter fought alongside the British in the war. In 1783, when Great Britain surrendered at the hands of the American revolutionaries, tens of thousands of Loyalists took refuge in Canada. Between 5,000 and 6,000 moved to the virgin lands of the west, now Ontario, founding the first permanent colonies in that region. Most, however, settled along the north shore of the St. Lawrence River and Lake Ontario.

In 1791, London promulgated the Constitutional Act, which divided Canada into two provinces, Lower Canada (Québec) and Upper Canada (Ontario). Lower Canada, which included the territory settled by the French, remained subject to French civil law, while Upper Canada, located west of the Ottawa River and populated mainly by former Loyalists, was subject to English common law.

Bytown

In the years following the American Revolution, the colonists of Upper Canada regarded their neighbours to the south with distrust, and with good reason. In 1812, claiming to be tired of Britain's strict control over the Great Lakes, the Americans declared war on that country and, consequently, on Canada. The Loyalists and their descendants still constituted the bulk of the population of Upper Canada, so emotions ran high. Great Britain, busy with the Napoleonic Wars in Europe, was unable to offer its colony much help. The settlers nonetheless managed to fend off the American attack, causing the United States to suffer the first military defeat in its brief history.

Though invasion had been narrowly avoided, this war illustrated how isolated Upper Canada was geographically. The rapids that hindered travel up the St. Lawrence River in many places made the colony vulnerable in times of war and limited trade in times of peace. To improve the situation, canals were dug in several places along the St. Lawrence, notably in Lachine (1814) and Welland (1824).

Fear of a new conflict with the Americans also prompted British authorities to dig a third canal, the Rideau Canal, linking the Ottawa River to Fort Henry (Kingston). In this way, maritime traffic could avoid sailing up the very vulnerable section of the Saint Lawrence River that ran alongside the American border. Not everyone approved of this project, however; the governments of Upper and Lower Canada, preoccupied with the construction of the Welland and Lachine Canals, were not in favour of colossal sums being spent on digging a new waterway. They were opposed by the British government, which considered the Rideau Canal to be a military necessity. In 1825, abandoning all hope of obtaining any financial contribution from the two other governments, the British began construction.

Portrait

Back in 1823, Governor Dalhousie had purchased 160 hectares of land for the British Crown on the south shore of the Ottawa River, opposite Wrightown (present-day Hull), a small farming community founded by Philemon Wright in 1800. It was here that construction began on the canal in 1826, under the supervision of Lieutenant-Colonel By. A small village developed, inhabited by labourers who had come to dig the canal and officials sent to oversee the project. It was named Bytown after the Lieutenant-Colonel.

Colonel By statue

The British government, which owned a good portion of the land around the canal, also charged Governor Dalhousie and Lieutenant-Colonel By with developing the territory, and policies encouraging settlers to the region were adopted. These policies reflected the values of the two men: affluent English officials interested in leasing property were offered excellent terms and awarded the best lands, those located west of the canal, which became Upper Town. A few shopkeepers, workers and lumberjacks, mainly French-speaking or Irish Catholics, took up residence on the east shore of the canal, where the land, though not as desirable, had been drained in 1827, creating Lower Town. These two groups had radically different points of view and rarely agreed on anything, so the development of the town was accompanied by much dissension.

It was impossible to oppose this arrangement, since there were only three landowners: the British government and two individuals: Nicholas Sparks owned about 80ha—a good portion of Upper Town—which afforded him a substantial income, while Louis Besserer owned land on the east bank of the canal, which he later subdivided.

Bytown 1830-1850

In Bytown's early years, authorities viewed agriculture as the key to the region's economic development. However, due to the local climate and geology (the acidic soil of the mixed forest), harvests were not as abundant as expected. In fact, the land was ill-suited to agriculture. Gradually, local residents gave up on farming and turned to the forest, which seemed like another possible source of income.

The canal, completed in 1832, did not serve its intended purpose either. Yes, it was a new waterway, but it definitely would not be as useful as hoped. Its large number of locks made it a slow and expensive route. The cost was that much higher because the merchants of Montréal and Kingston set the lock fees as they pleased. Furthermore, since there were no more conflicts between Canada and the United States, the canal never served its primary, military function.

It was thus the forest that enabled Bytown to attain a certain level of prosperity. Many residents became lumberjacks, either as their sole source of income or to offset poor harvests. Though many people earned their living cutting down trees, it was the transportation of the logs that truly enabled the town to flourish. Once chopped

down, the trees were floated to Montréal on the Ottawa River. En route, the raftsmen (*draveurs* in French) had to confront a sizable obstacle: the Chaudière Falls, on the outskirts of Bytown. Since they had no choice but to stop and take apart their rafts, they would take the opportunity to stock up on supplies at the same time. Many businesses sprang up to meet their needs. In 1841, Bytown had 3,000 inhabitants at the most, but no fewer than 38 shops; within four years, that number had risen to 51.

Though the lumber industry enabled many residents to earn a living, it did not provide much economic stability, as prices fluctuated according to demand. A drop in the price of wood, such as occurred in 1846, inevitably caused a depression in Bytown, prompting many people to leave. In short, the lumber industry enabled many people to survive but made few rich.

The vulnerable local economy, combined with the long-term lease policies established by the administration, also affected Bytown's appearance. In the 1850s, nothing was really built to last, aside from a few government buildings and a handful of large, opulent residences in Upper

Town. The town was essentially a collection of flimsy little wooden houses. Furthermore, it was not developing around a single centre of activity, but rather in two parts, Upper Town and Lower Town, which seemed to be constantly at odds with one another.

This opposition was a source of tension, particularly between the various religious groups, namely the Catholics, who made up 58% of the population of Bytown and lived in Lower Town, and the Protestant minority who lived in Upper Town and were supported by area farmers. Conflicts also existed within the Catholic community, which was not a homogenous group. Irish and French descendents, who were frequently competing for the same jobs, often had violent altercations. The source of this rivalry lay in each individual's desire to improve his or her own lot. In the early 1850s, Bytown had only a few thousand inhabitants, who were too concerned with survival to envision the unusual fate that awaited their town.

From Small Town to Capital

In 1840, the colonies of Lower and Upper Canada were joined under the Act of Union. The following year, Kingston, a small military garrison that had become a bustling town thanks to the canals on the St. Lawrence River, was chosen to be the seat of Parliament. Not everyone was pleased with this choice, however. Toronto, Montréal and Québec all felt slighted. Furthermore, Kingston's proximity to the United States and the never-ending fear of an American invasion put the British government ill at ease. Parliament was moved to Montréal two years later, then back to Kingston in 1849. The time had clearly come to settle on one safe, neutral place to establish the government.

Bytown was also examining its options during this period, with many local residents looking for ways to promote its growth. The arrival of the railroad, which revolutionized the transportation of merchandise, gave them hope that their town would become a regional railway hub. It didn't take them long to figure out that this was not going to happen, since Bytown was not located on the communication route between Montréal and Toronto. Efforts were made, however, to link the town to the American market by laying out a railway line between Bytown and

The Union Bridge

The Chaudière Falls were the key factor in the development of Ottawa and Hull. In the early days, they forced rafters to disassemble the wooden rafts they used to travel down the Ottawa River, and to stop in the towns on the river's shore. In addition, the falls allowed for the construction of a number of mills. But they were also a sizeable obstacle between the two towns, hindering communication. As a result, the idea came about early on of building a bridge that would connect the towns and, in a way, become a link between Upper and Lower Canada.

The bridge was constructed between 1826 and 1828, and required a fair amount of imagination on the part of its designers, since the river is quite wide at its location, and the falls tumultuous. The bridge was made of seven sections, each one crossing the river and ending on one of the Ottawa River's islands. The longest section measured nearly 213ft (65m). After part of the structure collapsed in 1843, it was rebuilt as a suspended bridge. Today, the Chaudière Bridge has replaced the Union Bridge. Other bridges were also added throughout the years, such as the Portage, Alexandra and Macdonald-Cartier bridges, which cross the river and allow commuters to travel from one city to the other.

Portrait

Prescott. Unfortunately, this inefficient line took years to build and gobbled up a fortune in the process.

The Chaudière Falls offered a better means of sprucing up the local economy. Toward the 1850s, sawmills were built at the foot of the falls, but it wasn't until 1853 that the Crown, which owned Victoria Island, started selling off plots of land for the construction of mills that truly capitalized on the falls' potential as a source of energy. The sale of these lands enabled entrepreneurs like Harris and Bronson to build a mill. Blasdell, Currier and Co., which owned a mill at the foot of the falls, took the opportunity to increase their capacity. Finally, a third player came on the scene: Philip Thompson, who built saw, flour, oat and carding mills, as well as a spinning mill on Chaudière Island. Even though ownership of these mills soon passed into the hands of rich American businessmen, who invested the major part of their profits in their own country, Bytown still enjoyed a definite economic boost.

While the economy of Bytown was taking shape, the powers that ruled United Canada were focussing their efforts on finding the perfect location for their capital. Though Montréal, Toronto, Kingston and Québec City were all vying for the honour, Bytown appealed to many people. In fact, though some saw it as a drab, violent place, it had a lot of advantages: it was at the border of what used to be Upper and Lower Canada; it had an equal number of French- and English-speaking residents, and the British government owned pieces of land there that would provide perfect sites for government buildings. For these reasons, and also because the choice was less politically controversial, Macdonald and Cartier's Liberal-Conservative party favoured Bytown. To get their way, these two men demanded that the decision be made by the executive branch of the government; it is highly unlikely that this poor little town would have become the capital of United Canada if democracy had come into play. In 1857, Bytown, renamed Ottawa, officially became the capital.

The Development of Ottawa

Ottawa residents could not have hoped for more. Colossal sums were immediately allotted for the Parliament Buildings. Construction began in 1859, creating an employment boom and thus attracting scores of workers and merchants to the area. Though the project did not always go smoothly, Parliament was able to hold its first session in 1866 in a partially finished building. The following year, the Dominion of Canada was created. Originally, this confederation was made up of four provinces: New Brunswick, Nova Scotia, Québec (formerly Lower Canada) and Ontario (formerly Upper Canada). One day, however, the Dominion of Canada would stretch from the Atlantic to the Pacific, with Ottawa as its capital.

The splendid Gothic Revival buildings that house the Parliament and the city's major government institutions began to dominate Ottawa's urban landscape, along with the steeples of the various local churches. However, a number of neighbourhoods were in a pitiful state; wooden houses were often destroyed by fire, the dirt roads became impassable during the spring thaw, the drainage system was inadequate, and sanitary conditions needed to be improved throughout the city. A lot of work needed to be done.

The city began to undergo a transformation in the late 1860s, when it became clear that its drainage system had to be modernized. However, it was only after a clear assessment of exactly what the city required and a lengthy evaluation of all possible solutions that construction was finally begun in the late 1870s. This new drainage system also led to the creation of an efficient fire brigade. Electricity, which started to become available in Ottawa around 1885, also helped shape the capital's new face, as certain streets, notably Sparks and Sussex, were equipped with streetlamps, and streetcars gradually replaced horse-drawn vehicles. Finally, a police force was set up to keep a curb on violence.

Another aspect of Ottawa's transformation in the second half of the 19th century was its expansion; several parts of town grew considerably such as Lebreton, an industrial sector by the Chaudière Falls, and Lower Town. This expansion was partly the result of the government's decision to start selling land in the 1850s. New parts of town were also developed. Louis Besserer's land in the area known as Sandy Hill was subdivided so that elegant new houses could be built there.

All these changes, combined with new employment opportunities, at-

Portrait

tracted scores of newcomers, and the population of the city more than doubled at the end of the 19th century. This metamorphosis did not, however, alter the social fabric, which still contained great rifts. Lower Town, gradually abandoned by the Irish community in favour of other parts of Ottawa, became a bastion of the Francophone population, prompting French-speakers to take action to protect their rights, particularly the right to be educated in French. Over the years, however, the power of the Francophones was eclipsed by that of the wealthy Anglophone communities of Upper Town, whose members had many of the most prestigious and best-paying jobs in town. Furthermore, the Anglophone community never seemed to stop growing. Another area, Sandy Hill, expanded rapidly and also came to play a prominent role in the city's evolution. It was different from the other two neighbourhoods in that it was home to Catholics and Protestants of all different origins. Most residents belonged to a new group: the city's well-to-do political elite.

The 20th Century and Modernity

At the dawn of the 20th century, Ottawa's fate seemed extremely promising, since it was closely linked to that of Canada, which was entering a period of tremendous economic growth at the time. The nation's optimistic prime minister, Sir Wilfrid Laurier, predicted that the 20th century belonged to Canada, and therefore, to Ottawa. Laurier was convinced that Ottawa was destined for a brilliant future, thanks to the growth of its paper and manufacturing industries. He also reintroduced the idea of digging a canal between Ottawa and Georgian Bay.

Laurier's hopes soon faded once it became evident that local industries could only expand so much. Be that as it may, Ottawa, whose civil service was constantly growing, continued to bustle with activity.

Ottawa's expansion also involved a substantial increase in the local population, which passed the 110,000 mark during World War I. Given the city's now considerable size, authorities were forced to tackle various issues related to urbanization and public health, with water treatment and health care facilities at the top of the list.

From 1929 to 1945, Canada's economic, political and social structure was severely disrupted by two international events, the economic crisis and World War II. The Great Depression of the 1930s halted Canada's economic growth. In Ottawa, as everywhere else in the country, a large portion of the population became unemployed. The government offered little assistance, and the jobless were left to fend for themselves. Poverty quickly set in, which was so serious that in 1933 an unemployment programme administered by the Public Welfare Department had to be set up, thus heralding the creation of the welfare state.

World War II led to an explosion in the number of civil servants in Ottawa, which increased from 12,000 (1939) to 36,000 (1945) in the space of six years. Later, as the Canadian government adopted a more and more interventionist stance domestically, the civil service continued to grow, reaching its peak in the 1970s.

With the expansion of the federal government and the resulting increase in the number of civil servants, the city grew at lightning speed. There was a construction boom in such areas as government buildings, big commercial buildings and housing developments, which transformed certain neighbourhoods and pushed the city limits ever outwards. The city's layout, which authorities had unsuccessfully attempted to redesign at various times during the first half of 20th century, started to take a definite shape in the 1960s. Since then, the city has been in a state of constant improvement.

Politics

The British North America Act of 1867, the constitutional document that forms the basis of Canadian Confederation, divides power between two levels of government. Besides the federal government in Ottawa, each of the ten Canadian provinces, including Ontario, elect their own governments with the power to legislate in certain areas. Based on the British model, the political systems in Canada and Ontario give legislative power to parliaments elected by universal suffrage. The political party with the greatest number of elected members forms the government except in very rare cases when very close results enable the government to be formed by a

Portrait

coalition between the second-place and third-place parties.

Elections are usually held every four years, but a government can prolong its mandate for up to five years. Unlike the system in the United States, the party in power decides on the timing of elections, which are based on a simple majority in single-member constituencies. As in Britain, this usually leads to battles between only two strong parties.

On the federal scene, two political parties, the Liberal Party and the Progressive Conservative Party, have traditionally taken turns governing Canada ever since Confederation in 1867. The current Canadian prime minister, Jean Chrétien, was elected under the Liberal banner in 1993 and again in 1997. He succeeded Conservative Prime Minister Brian Mulroney, who had won the 1984 and 1988 federal elections before giving up his post to the party's new leader Kim Campbell near the end of his second mandate.

In Canadian political history, the 1993 federal election was doubtless a watershed, for it led to an unprecedented realignment of the political spectrum. The Conservatives and New Democrats (the traditional third party) were nearly wiped out and two new parties, the Bloc Québécois and the Reform Party (henceforth the Canadian Alliance) gained significant representation in Parliament.

As for provincial politics, the Conservative Party has traditionally held sway in Ontario. In fact, between 1943 and 1985, the province was governed without interruption by Conservative premiers. Although they have had to make compromises, especially at times of minority governments, the Conservatives have never been very warm to the idea of promoting the interests of women, the poor or minorities such as the numerous French-speaking people in the northern part of the province. The 1985 election put an end to the long Conservative reign in Ontario, though the results still favoured the Conservatives, who won 52 seats against 48 for the Liberals and 25 for the New Democrats. It took a coalition between David Peterson's Liberals and Bob Rae's New Democrats to end nearly a half-century of Conservative rule in Ontario.

Peterson became premier of the province and enacted a proactive law on equal wages for women. Two important matters greatly reduced his popularity with the electorate, however. One was the Free Trade Agreement with the United States. The other was the Meech Lake Accord, which sought to offer Québec a special status within the Canadian Confederation but which two provinces failed to ratify. Peterson was opposed to the Free Trade Agreement but could not persuade the federal government to back off on this deal that a majority of Ontarians saw as unfavourable to their province's economic development. As for Meech Lake, which eventually fell through, Peterson gave it his support despite opposition from many people in Ontario.

Peterson was beaten in the 1990 provincial election but, to almost everyone's surprise, he was replaced by the New Democrats, lead by a brilliant intellectual, Bob Rae. During their years in coalition with the Liberals, Rae and his party had succeeded in ridding the party of its left-wing image, thereby winning the confidence of many Ontarians. Rae's five years as premier turned out to be very difficult, however, because of a harsh economic recession which lead to an increase in the province's debt.

Like his predecessor, Rae was to hold power for only five years. In 1995, he was replaced by Mike Harris of the Conservative Party, whose platform was essentially to fight tooth and nail against the deficit through radical cuts in government services.

Economy

The economy of the Ottawa region is largely dependent on the federal civil service, which, both directly and indirectly, employs a large percentage of the local workforce. Generally speaking, the civil service provides stability in the employment sector and also allows for a particularly large middle class. The annual household income, furthermore, is above the national average. This traditional stability has been threatened somewhat in recent years by government cutbacks aiming to reduce the federal deficit. The service sector also provides jobs, particularly in the computer and insurance industries. The Rideau Valley is still the area best-suited to farming in the Ottawa region, and the forest industry continues to play a major role in the economy, especially on the Québec side.

Portrait

Arts

In 50 years, Bytown grew from a small community of a few thousand people to a sizable city, leading to a major growth in its population. This metamorphosis brought about extensive changes in the town, which saw the construction of handsome government buildings and then the improvement of its public services. All this activity also had an impact on the local arts scene, which was gradually taking shape.

The mid-19th century saw the flowering of the arts scene in both the francophone and anglophone communities, whose cultural institutions developed at the same time. In the anglophone community, this flowering manifested itself primarily in the creation of various organizations, such as The Mechanics Institute and Athenaeum (1853), The Natural History Society of Ottawa (1863) and The Ottawa Field Naturalists Club, which later became The Arts and Letters Club. All three contributed to the community's cultural vitality.

The Institut Canadien Français d'Ottawa, run by a religious order in those days, was the centre of musical, theatrical and literary activity in the francophone community. This institute later became the Collège d'Ottawa and the Université d'Ottawa. This group of French-speaking intellectuals, led by local religious communities, soon focussed on defending the rights of francophones. The creation of a French-language education system, directed by Catholic communities, was among their demands. This subject caused a great deal of controversy, since it put the anglophone Catholic community in a quandary. A serious social debate ensued. In order to defend their views, the francophones founded a newspaper, *Le Droit*, in 1913. In 1918, the two communities reached a compromise; the administration of primary schools would be divided between English- and French-speaking Catholics. It wasn't until 1968, however, that the Ontario government agreed to create public high schools for French-language education. Prior to that, the religious communities had established private schools, so only a privileged few had access to education in french.

Though the city's communities were constantly in conflict, right from the start there was a common desire to equip Ottawa with cultural institutions worthy of a national capital. In 1894, the city's first symphony orchestra, composed mainly of amateur musicians, was founded, but they like many of the other little groups that emerged on the arts scene around that time, it succumbed to financial difficulties eight years later. It was succeeded by other orchestras, but they all met similar fates. It wasn't until many years later that any real effort was made to develop the city's cultural scene. Finally, in 1965-1966, the Ottawa Symphony Orchestra was founded. The fact that it was so difficult, if not impossible, to find a venue in which to perform prevented many smaller orchestras and theatre companies from flourishing. Only the Ottawa Little Theatre, founded in 1912, managed to find a home and survive; they are still performing popular plays to this day. The construction of the National Arts Centre in 1969 was a milestone. Devoted to the performing arts, this centre has three theatres, where top-quality plays, dance performances and concerts given by the house orchestra are presented. The capital area also lays claim to several prestigious museums, including the Canadian Museum of Civilization, in Hull, and the National Gallery of Canada, which have been instrumental in drawing attention to Canadian artists and culture.

Architecture

When Ottawa was founded in 1827, it had only been about 50 years since British colonists fleeing the newly independent United States settled west of the Ottawa River, in Ontario. These new arrivals, confronting a vast, almost virgin territory, preserved their architectural traditions; Georgian houses made of hewn stone, built according to a very specific, symmetrical design, gradually appeared on the horizon. These lovely houses still grace the Ottawa Valley. Though few remain in Ottawa, some examples can still be found, one being Louis Besserer's house (see p 90). Buildings dating back to the city's beginnings are rare. Aside from a few impressive projects like the Rideau Canal, little back then was built to last.

Rigorous adhesion to the Georgian style was gradually abandoned in favour of various styles inspired by trends of the past. Though very different from one another, these styles all emerged during the reign of Queen Victoria (1837-1901) and thus are all lumped together under the heading

Portrait

of "Victorian architecture." This was an important period in the history of Ottawa, which was named the capital of United Canada in 1857, then of Canada in 1867; with this change of status, the city began to undergo a transformation.

Though Gothic Revival was the most popular style of the second half of the 19th century, other styles, notably Queen Anne, distinguished by gables, dormer windows and asymmetrical lines, emerged in residential architecture.

Earnscliffe

Though a few handsome Gothic Revival buildings had already been erected along the Ottawa River (Earnscliffe, see p 93), the construction of the Parliament Buildings set off a rage for this style, characterized by Gothic arches, pinnacles and crenellations. During the second half of the 19th century, the Gothic Revival style was used for many government buildings and churches; indeed, to some extent, it shaped the face of the capital.

The Second Empire style, associated with Parisian sophistication under Napoleon III and characterized by the use of mansard roofs, among other features, was also used for a number of public buildings (Langevin Block, see p 76).

In the 20th century, Victorian architecture remained in fashion but was toned down. Then, little by little, another style emerged to change the face of the capital once again: the Château style was inspired by French châteaux of the 14th and 15th centuries, particularly those of the Loire Valley. The first building in Ottawa designed in this style was the Château Laurier, erected on the banks of the Ottawa River in 1912. This aesthetic quickly gained favour with the federal government, which believed that it reflected just the right image for the nation's capital. A number of government buildings went up in the first few years of the 20th century. In order to make them blend in harmoniously with existing buildings, they were designed in an original combination of the Château and Gothic Revival styles, lending the city a distinctive appearance (Confederation Building, see p 77).

As Ottawa entered the modern era, newer architectural trends gradually emerged. Among these was the Art Deco style, used, most prominently, for banks and other financial institutions. Adaptations of that style can also be found; the Supreme Court of Canada, for example, features a blend of the Art Deco and Chateau styles.

The 1960s marked another turning point for the city. Not only were the roads redesigned to improve the flow of traffic around the Rideau Canal, but thanks to a new law, it was now permissible to erect buildings taller than those of Parliament. Bit by bit, concrete, glass and steel skyscrapers appeared on the skyline—not always embellishing it. In the 1980s, the beautification of the nation's capital became a central concern, and a program was launched to achieve that end, by creating new parks and erecting magnificent buildings like the National Gallery of Canada and the Canadian Museum of Civilization.

A Few Famous Ontarians

After serving in the British army against France and Spain, **George Ramzay Dalhousie** (1770-1838) came to Canada to serve in Nova Scotia. His main claim to fame was as governor of British North America from 1820 to 1828. We have Dalhousie to thank for the Rideau Canal, since it was he who, in 1823, purchased 160 hectares of land west of the Rideau River and south of the Ottawa River so that the canal could be dug. In a way, he is the father of Ottawa.

Lieutenant-Colonel **John By** (1779-1836) entered military academy in 1797. In 1802, he was sent to Canada,

Portrait

where he helped build the locks on the St. Lawrence River and the fortifications of Québec City. In 1811, he returned to England to fight Spain and France. In 1826, this brilliant, seasoned engineer, who was 47 at the time, was called back to Canada and placed in charge of the construction of the Rideau Canal. In addition to supervising this project, he furthered the development of the little village taking shape on this site, which was named Bytown in his honour. Despite these efforts, his career ended on a regrettable note: when the canal ended up going way over budget, he was called back to England to answer accusations that he had mismanaged the funds.

A poor Irish immigrant, **Nicholas Sparks** first settled in Wrightown (now Hull), where he worked as a farmer. In 1821, he bought 80 hectares of relatively worthless land covered with trees and stones on the south bank of the Ottawa River for the sum of 95 pounds. When he made this purchase, he had no idea how much the land would increase in value. A few years later, the Rideau Canal was dug right alongside his vast piece of property. As Bytown developed, Sparks got rich leasing out plots of land. He is also known for his many efforts to encourage economic growth in Upper Town, which had developed on his land.

Only one other person owned land alongside the Rideau Canal, on the east side. **Louis Besserer** did not play as prominent a role as Sparks, since he did not subdivide his land until the second half of the 19th century, when Ottawa, by then the nation's capital, was booming.

John A. Macdonald (1815-1891) was elected to the Legislative Assembly of United Canada for the first time in 1844, then re-elected in 1848, 1851, 1854, 1857, 1861 and 1863. Starting in 1864, he played a vital role in the creation of the Canadian Confederation. In 1867, he was elected the first federal prime minister. Except for 1875, when his government had to step down in the wake of a scandal, he held that office until his death in 1891.

Wilfrid Laurier (1841-1919), a Liberal, was first elected to federal office in 1874. He was appointed a minister in 1878 and became leader of the opposition in 1887. A great speaker and negotiator, he was the first French Canadian to be elected prime minister of Canada.

Even in his first years in office, he had great plans for Ottawa, which he wanted to make the "Washington of the North." During his terms as prime minister, considerable efforts were made to beautify the capital, with no fewer than 11 stately buildings going up, among them the Château Laurier, the Royal Canadian Mint and the Connaught Building. He lived in Ottawa right up until his death, and his house is open to the public (see p 92).

William Lyon Mackenzie King (1874-1950) succeeded Wilfrid Laurier as leader of the Liberal Party in 1919. A Doctor of Political Science, he spent part of his career in the civil service, specializing in labour-related issues. Prime minister of Canada from 1921 to 1930 and from 1935 to 1948, he, like Laurier, was keen on beautifying the nation's capital. To that end, he persuaded the Public Works Department to use the Château style for government buildings. His summer home in Kingsmere is open to the public (see p 107).

Architect **Thomas Fuller** (1823-1898), a native of England, started his career in Canada, in Toronto, where he joined forces with Chilion Jones. Both men soon earned themselves a

solid reputation, particularly in the domain of church construction. In 1859, their design was selected for the main building on Parliament Hill in Ottawa. In 1881, Fuller was named head architect of the Department of Public Works. He was responsible for erecting some 140 buildings across the country and could thus be said to have shaped the face of Canada in his day.

David Ewart (1843-1921) was the head architect at the Department of Public Works from 1897 to 1914. He was in charge of erecting numerous government buildings all over the country, and several others in the capital, most notably the Royal Canadian Mint and the building that now houses the Canadian War Museum.

In 1882, **Archibald Lampman** (1861-1899) received a diploma in classics and joined the civil service as a clerk for the post office department in Ottawa. A great observer of nature who developed a personal style influenced by the Romantic movement, he was one of the greatest Canadian poets of the late 19th century. He died young, having published only two collections of poems, *Among the Millet* (1888) and *Lyrics of Earth* (1895); a third, *Alcyone and*

Other Poems was about to come out when he passed away.

Duncan Campbell Scott (1862-1947), a friend of Archibald Lampman's, also worked in the civil service in Ottawa, for the Ministry of Indian Affairs. Upon Lampman's advice, Scott also devoted himself to writing. In the course of his lengthy career, he published short stories, novels and essays but remains best known as a poet.

Margaret Atwood (1939-) spent her early childhood in Ottawa. Her family moved to Toronto when she was seven, and she has since lived in a number of North American cities, including Boston, Montréal and Vancouver. A talented poet, critic, novelist and short story writer, she has created a very personal body of work. In 1965, she won Canada's most important literary prize, the Governor General's Award, for *The Circle Game*, a collection of poems. A prolific author, she has since published about 20 other works, many of which have enjoyed great success. Her work is marked by a critical, sometimes satirical view of society and an activist stance in regard to feminism and various other causes. Atwood has also earned a name for herself as a television writer, having been involved in a number of series. Among her numerous other accomplishments and honours, Atwood was recently awarded Britain's prestigious Booker Prize for her outstanding new novel, *The Blind Assassin*.

The popular singer and songwriter **Paul Anka** (1941-) has recorded a number of hit songs, such as *You Are My Destiny*, and composed many others for such renowned fellow artists as Frank Sinatra (*My Way*). With more than 400 songs to his name, he was one of the most famous Canadian singers and songwriters in the world in his heyday.

Bruce Cockburn (1945-) was born in Ottawa and spent a good part of his childhood on a farm in the area. This experience stayed with him, and his feelings about rural life are reflected in the lyrics of his early albums. Influenced as a child by rock legends like Elvis Presley, Bob Dylan and John Lennon, Cockburn later studied harmony and composition at the Berkeley School of Music in Boston, then spent some time performing on the streets of Paris before returning to his home town. In the late 1960s, he adopted a much more acoustic sound, which he never abandoned. To date, this pop star has recorded about 20 albums and has received countless awards for his music.

Born in Ottawa to a French Canadian father and a Hungarian mother, **Alanis Nadine Morissette** (1974-) is one of the most successful Canadian singers of the 1990s. Her first album, recorded when she was just 17, won the Juno Award for most promising female singer. Though already off to a good start, she attained true celebrity status in 1995, at the age of 21, with her album *Jagged Little Pill*, which won all sorts of awards, including the coveted Grammy for album of the year.

Dan Aykroyd (1952-) was born in Ottawa, where his parents, Peter Samuel Gilbert and Lorraine Gougeon, were federal civil servants. He spent his entire youth in Ottawa and even enrolled in university here. He began his career as a comedian in Canada before becoming a star as a member of the cast of the American television show *Saturday Night Live*. He later appeared in a number of popular American movies, including *The Blues Brothers* (1980), *Ghostbusters* (1984) and *Spies Like Us* (1985). Despite his success in the U.S., he has continued to work on television projects for the Canadian Broadcasting Corporation.

Wd.Pierson

Practical Information

Information in this chapter will help you to better plan your trip, not only well in advance, but once you've arrived in Ottawa.

Important details on entrance formalities and other procedures, as well as general information, have been compiled for visitors from other countries as well as Canadians.

Ottawa's **area code** is *613*; that of Hull is *819*.

Entrance Formalities

Passports

A valid passport is usually sufficient for most visitors planning to stay less than three months; visas are not required. A three month extension is possible, but a return ticket and proof of sufficient funds to cover this extension may be required.

Caution: some countries do not have an agreement with Canada concerning health and accident insurance, so it is advisable to have the appropriate coverage. For more information, see the section entitled **"Health"** on page 56.

Extended Visits

Visitors must submit a request to extend their visit **in writing** and **before** the expiration of their visa (the date is usually written in your passport) to an Immigration Canada office. To make a request you must have a valid passport, a return ticket, proof of sufficient funds to cover the stay, as well as the $65 non-refundable filing-fee. In some cases (work, study), however, the request must be made **before** arriving in Canada.

Embassies and Consulates

Canadian Embassies and Consulates Abroad

AUSTRALIA
Canadian Consulate General
Level 5, Quay West, 111 Harrington Rd., Sydney, N.S.W., Australia 2000
☎ *(612) 364-3000*
⇌ *(612) 364-3098*

BELGIUM
Canadian Embassy
2 Avenue de Tervuren, 1040 Brussels Métro Mérode
☎ *(02) 735.06.40*
⇌ *(02) 735.06.09*

DENMARK
Canadian Embassy
Kr. Bernikowsgade 1, DK=1105 Copenhagen K, Denmark
☎ /⇌ *33.48.32.00*

FINLAND
Canadian Embassy
Pohjos Esplanadi 25 B, 00100 Helsinki, Finland
☎ *(9) 171-141*
⇌ *(9) 601-060*

GERMANY
Canadian Consulate General
Internationales Handelzentrum, Friedrichstrasse 95, 23rd Floor, 10117 Berlin, Germany
☎ *(30) 261.11.61*
⇌ *(30) 262.92.06*

GREAT BRITAIN
Canada High Commission
Macdonald House, One Grosvenor Square, London W1X 0AB, England
☎ *(171) 258-6600*
⇌ *(171) 258-6384*

ITALY
Canadian Embassy
Via G.B. de Rossi 27, 00161 Rome
☎ *(6) 44.59.81*
⇌ *(6) 44.59.87*

NETHERLANDS
Canadian Embassy
Parkstraat 25, 2514JD The Hague Netherlands
☎ *(70) 361-4111*
⇌ *(70) 365-6283*

NORWAY
Canadian Embassy
Wergelandsveien 7, Oslo 1244, Norway
☎ *(47) 46.69.55*
⇌ *(47) 69.34.67*

SPAIN
Canadian Embassy
Edificio Goya, Calle Nuñez de
Balboa 35, 28001 Madrid
☎*(1) 431.43.00*
⇌*(1) 431.23.67*

SWEDEN
Canadian Embassy
Tegelbacken 4, 7th floor, Box 16129
10323 Stockholm, Sweden
☎*(8) 613-9900*
⇌*(8) 24.24.91*

SWITZERLAND
Canadian Embassy
Kirchenfeldstrasse 88, 3000 Berne 6
☎*(31) 352.63.81*
⇌*(31) 352.73.15*

UNITED STATES
Canadian Embassy
501 Pennsylvania Ave., N.W., Washington, DC, 20001
☎*(202) 682-1740*
⇌*(202) 682-7726*

Canadian Consulate General
1175 Peachtree St. NE, 100 Colony
Square Suite 1700, Atlanta, Georgia
30361
☎*(404) 532-2000*
⇌*(404) 532-2050*

Canadian Consulate General
Three Copley Pl., Suite 400, Boston,
Massachusetts, 02116
☎*(617) 262-3760*
⇌*(617) 262-3415*

Canadian Consulate General
Two Prudential Plaza, 180 N. Stetson
Ave., Suite 2400, Chicago, Illinois
60601
☎*(312) 616-1860*
⇌*(312) 616-1877*

Canadian Consulate General
St. Paul Place, 750 N. St. Paul St.,
Suite 1700, Dallas, Texas, 75201
☎*(214) 922-9806*
⇌*(214) 922-9815*

Canadian Consulate General
600 Renaissance Center, Suite 1100,
Detroit, Michigan, 48234-1798
☎*(313) 567-2085*
⇌*(313) 567-2164*

Canadian Consulate General
550 South Hope St., 9th Floor, Los
Angeles, California, 90071
☎*(213) 347-2700*
⇌*(213) 620-8827*

Canadian Consulate General
Suite 900, 701 Fourth Ave. S., Minne-
apolis, Minnesota, 55415-1899
☎*(612) 333-4641*
⇌*(612) 332-4061*

Canadian Consulate General
1251 Ave. of the Americas, New York,
New York, 10020-1175
☎*(212) 596-1600*
⇌*(212) 596-1793*

Canadian Consulate General
One Marine Midland Center, Suite
3000, Buffalo, New York, 14203-2884
☎*(716) 852-1247*
⇌*(716) 852-4340*

Canadian Consulate General
412 Plaza 600, Sixth and Stewart sts.
Seattle, Washington, 98101-1286
☎*(206) 442-1777*
⇌*(206) 443-1782*

Practical
Information

Foreign Embassies in Ottawa

AUSTRALIA
Australian High Commission
50 O'Connor St., 7th floor Suite 710
Ottawa, ON, K1P 6L2
☎236-0841
⇄236-4376

BELGIUM
Embassy
80 Elgin St., Suite 401, Ottawa, ON
K1P 1B7
☎236-7267
⇄236-7882

DENMARK
Embassy
47 Clarence St., Suite 450, Ottawa
ON, K1N 9K1
☎562-1811
⇄562-1812

FINLAND
Embassy
55 Metcalfe, Suite 850, Ottawa, ON
K1P 6L5
☎236-2389
⇄238-1474

GERMANY
Embassy
1 Waverley St., Ottawa, ON, K2P 0T8
☎232-1101
⇄594-9330

GREAT BRITAIN
British High Commission–Consular Section
80 Elgin, Ottawa, ON, K1P 5K7
☎237-2008
⇄237-6537

ITALY
Embassy
275 Slater Street, 21st Floor, Ottawa
ON, K1P 5H9
☎232-2401
⇄233-1484

NETHERLANDS
Embassy
350 Albert St., Suite 2020, Ottawa, ON
K1R 1A4
☎237-5030
⇄237-6471

NORWAY
Embassy
90 Sparks, Ottawa, Ont., K1P 5B4
☎238-6571

SPAIN
Embassy
74 Stanley Ave., Ottawa, ON, K1M 1P4
☎747-2252
⇄744-1224

SWEDEN
Embassy
377 Dalhousie St., Ottawa, ON
K1N 9N8
☎241-8553
⇄241-2277

SWITZERLAND
Embassy
5 Malborough Ave., Ottawa, ON
K1N 8E6
☎235-1837
⇄563-1394

UNITED STATES
Embassy
400 Sussex Dr., Ottawa, ON
K1N 1G8
☎238-5335
⇄238-5720

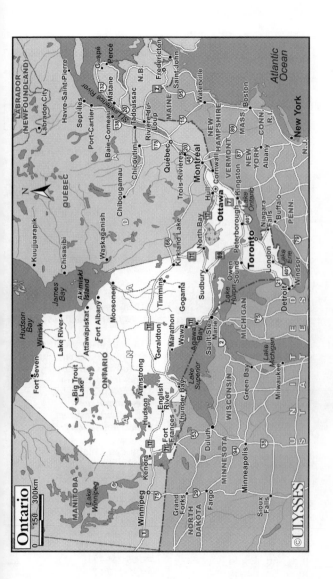

Customs

If you are bringing gifts into Canada, remember that certain restrictions apply. Smokers (minimum age is 16) can bring in a maximum of 200 cigarettes, 50 cigars, 400 grams of tobacco, or 400 tobacco sticks. For wine and alcohol the limit is 1.1 litres; in practice, however, two bottles per person are usually allowed. The limit for beer is twenty-four 355-ml size cans or bottles.

Plants, vegetation, and food: there are very strict rules regarding the importation of plants, flowers, and other vegetation; it is therefore not advisable to bring any of these types of products into the country. If it is absolutely necessary, contact the Customs-Agriculture service of the Canadian embassy **before** leaving your country.

Pets: if you are travelling with your pet, you will need a health certificate (available from your veterinarian) as well as a rabies vaccination certificate. It is important to remember that the vaccination must have been administered **at least** 30 days **before** your departure and should not be more than a year old.

Tax reimbursements for visitors: it is possible to be reimbursed for certain taxes paid on purchases made in Canada (see p 53).

Tourist Information

A tourist information office has just opened its doors a stone's throw from Parliament Hill. Brochures, information, a hotel-room reservation centre... all the services you could possibly need are available here.

Capital Call Centre
late May to early Sep, every day, 8:30am to 9pm; rest of the year, every day, 9am to 5pm
90 Wellington St.
☎*239-5000 or (800) 465-1867*

You can also obtain a great deal of additional tourist-related information by checking out various web sites. Here are a few:
www.capcan.ca
www.ottawakiosk.com
www.tourottawa.org

You can obtain tourist information on the Outaouais region by contacting:

Association Touristique de l'Outaouais
103 Rue Laurier
Hull, Québec
☎*(819) 778-2222*
☎*800-265-7822*
⇒*(819) 778-7758*
www.tourisme-outaouais.org

Tourist Offices Abroad

BELGIUM
Comission Canadienne du Tourisme
Rue Américaine 27, 1060 Bruxelles
☎*(2) 538-5792*
⇌*(2) 539-2433*

GERMANY
Canada Tourismusprogramm
Postfach 200 247, 63469 Maintal 2
Deutschland
☎*(49) 6181 45178*
⇌*6181 497558*
www.dfait-maeci.gc.ca/~bonn/To urism/eto2main.btm

GREAT BRITAIN
Visit Canada Centre
62-65 Trafalgar Square, London
WC2N 5DT
☎*891 715000 (calls charged at 50p/minute)*
⇌*(44) 171 389 1149*

Italy
Canadian Tourism Commission
Via Vittor Pisani 19, 20124 Milan
Italy
⇌*(2) 6758-3900*

NETHERLANDS
Canadian Tourism Commission
Sophialaan 7, 2514 JP, The Hague
Netherlands
⇌*(70) 3111682*

NORWAY
Geelmuyden. Kiese: Lilleakervn.2d
Postboks 362, N-1324 Lysaker
NORDICS
⇌*(47) 22 13 03 04*

SWITZERLAND
Welcome to Canada!
22, Freihofstrasse, 8700 Küsnacht
☎*(1) 910 90 01*
⇌*(1) 910 38 24*

UNITED STATES
Tour & Travel
84-03 Chapin Pkwy., Floor 3, Jamaica
Queens, New York 11432
☎*(718) 657-1727*
⇌*(718) 206-9114*

MC & IT
420 E. 55th St., New York, NY 10022
☎*(212) 317-1711*
⇌*(212) 317-1881*

Guided Tours

Those who are short of time but wish to get a good glimpse of the city's most attractive neighbourhoods can opt for a guided tour of Ottawa. A few companies offer worthwhile excursions through the streets of the capital.

Capital Double-Decker and Trolley Tours
$20
☎*749-3666 or (800) 823-6147*
www.ottawatour.com
Departures from next to the Capital Call Centre.

Amphibus "Lady Dive" Tours
☎*852-1132*
Gray Line
$16
☎*725-1441 or 800-440-0317*

Practical Information

The Phantoms of Ottawa

After discovering the streets of Ottawa by touring its museums and historic buildings, you might want to see another side of the Canadian capital. The Haunted Walk of Ottawa tourist agency offers a stroll though the city that introduces you to the historic ghosts and spirits that still haunt the city by night.

The Haunted Walk of Ottawa
$10
44 Sparks St.
☎*730-0575*

Getting to Ottawa

By Plane

Flights from major Canadian cities to Ottawa are frequent and reliable, but often expensive. Travellers leaving from Montreal might consider taking the train or the bus, which is sometimes faster (about a 2hr journey). From Europe, direct flights to Ottawa are rare; most stop first in either Montreal or Toronto.

Macdonald-Cartier Airport

Ottawa's international airport *(50 Airport Dr., ☎238-2000, ≈248-2003; www.ottawa-airport.ca)* is small, but welcomes several fights a day from other Canadian cities and different countries. It is located about 20min from downtown and can be easily reached by car (there are a number of car-rental companies here), by taxi or by bus (OC Transpo 96).

By car, you can reach downtown Ottawa via Airport Drive.

Airlines

Air Canada
☎*247-5000*

American Airlines
624 Bank St.
☎*(800) 624-5620*
≈*567-5609*

In Ontario

The **NorOntario** airline offers flights within the province to cities such as Sudbury,

Table of distances (km)
Via the shortest route

	Chicago (IL)	Hamilton	Kingston	Kitchener-Waterloo	London	Montréal	New York (NY)	Niagara Falls	Ottawa	Sault Ste. Marie	Sudbury	Toronto	Thunder Bay
Hamilton	788												
Kingston	1100	338											
Kitchener-Waterloo	767	69	369										
London	661	140	451	110									
Montréal	1383	621	299	650	738								
New York (NY)	1294	765	583	838	911	618							
Niagara Falls	896	77	408	156	227	689	690						
Ottawa	1242	480	203	511	600	202	719	544					
Sault Ste. Marie	780	748	894	777	699	1003	1498	814	806				
Sudbury	1079	460	609	490	572	700	1212	529	508	302			
Toronto	855	75	263	123	198	547	829	144	410	696	411		
Thunder Bay	1058	1469	1623	1496	1414	1638	2212	1534	1516	723	1019	1421	
Windsor/Detroit (MI)	460	318	626	306	191	912	1018	413	773	584	751	386	1310

Example: the distance between Montréal and Ottawa is 202 km.

Sault-Sainte-Marie, Thunder Bay and Timmins. It is a subsidiary of Air Canada; for more information, you can call one of the airline's offices or dial ☎*(705) 472-4500, ext. 358*.

By Train

VIA Rail transports passengers between the various Canadian provinces and serves several cities in southern and northern Ontario. This is without a doubt the most pleasant way of travelling from Montreal or Toronto to the capital. You will thus be treated to a comfortable ride and excellent service.

The Ottawa train station is located a few minutes by car from the downtown area and is served by a good road network and public transportation.

Ottawa Train Station
200 Tremblay Rd.
☎*244-8289 or 800-361-1235*

To get there by car, take the eastbound 417. The station is located a short distance past Riverside Drive.

Those opting for public transportation can take the OC Transpo's bus no. 95, which runs from the station to downtown, stopping

right near Parliament Hill. A ticket costs $2.25.

You can also take a taxi from the station. The ride downtown should cost you under $10.

The Routes

Modern and rapid (reaching up to 150 km/h), VIA Rail trains connect eastern Canadian cities in practically no time.

The Québec-Windsor corridor, one of the busiest routes, connects downtown Québec City, Montréal, Ottawa, Toronto, Windsor and other towns quickly and comfortably.

Economy or First Class?

Economy class carriages are equipped with comfortable seats and wide aisles and, for a slight surcharge, passengers can have something to eat as well. If you enjoy being waited on hand and foot, opt for first class, where the price of your ticket includes access to a waiting room, and priority boarding. You will also be served a meal, accompanied by wine and spirits as you relax in a comfortable seat, in warmly decorated carriages.

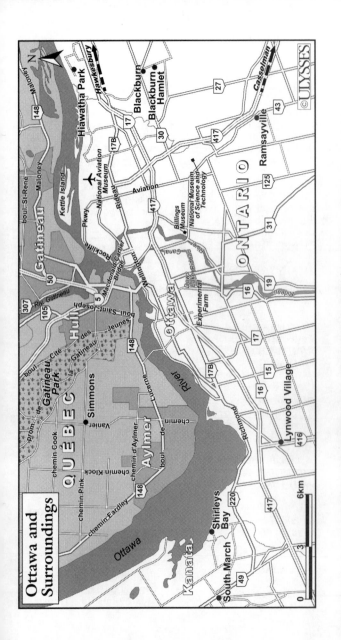

Ottawa and Surroundings

Some trains are equipped with a Skyline carriage in which a café and bar car allow you to enjoy yourself in the company of other passengers. These carriages have large panoramic windows that let you admire the passing landscape.

VIA offers several types of savings. For further information, call your travel agent or closest VIA office, or visit the website at: *www.viarail.ca*

You may also obtain information in your home country from the following agencies:

SWITZERLAND
Western Tours
☎*(01) 268 2323*
⇆*(01) 268 2373*

CANADA
☎*800-561-8630*
(or contact your travel agent)

AUSTRALIA
Asia Pacific/Walshes World
☎*(02) 9318 1044*
⇆*(02) 9318 2753*

ITALY
Gastaldi Tours
☎*(10) 24 511*
⇆*(10) 28 0354*

NETHERLANDS
Incento B.V.
☎*(035) 69 55111*
⇆*(035) 69 55155*

NEW ZEALAND
Walshes World
☎*(09) 379-3708*
⇆*(09) 309-0725*

UNITED KINGDOM
Leisurail
☎*01733-335-599*
⇆*01733-505-451*

UNITED STATES
☎*800-561-3949*
(or contact your travel agent)

By Bus

Extensive and inexpensive, buses travel to most points in Canada. Except for public transportation within cities, there is no government run service; several companies provide service throughout the country. Gray Coach, Greyhound and Voyageur Colonial all operate in the Ontario region.

Moreover, bus service, from Montreal and Toronto, is both rapid and punctual, and departures are frequent.

Ottawa Bus Station

265 Catherine St.
☎*238-5900*

From the bus station, you can get to the downtown area by bus (OC Transpo 4)

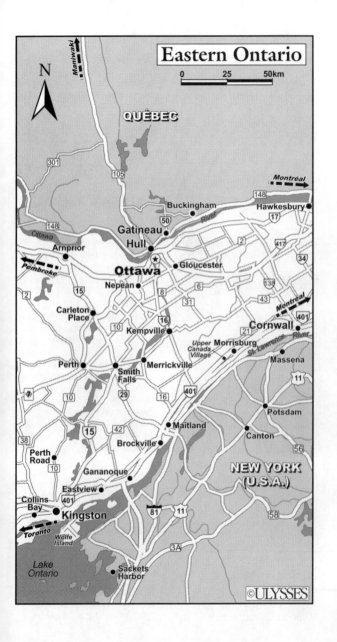

or by car via Kent or Bank streets.

Hull

238 Boul. Saint-Joseph
☎(819) 771-2442

Here are the addresses and phone numbers of some principal bus stations that have frequent departures to Hull:

Montréal
505 Boulevard De Maisonneuve Est
☎(514) 842-2281

Toronto
610 Bay St.
☎(416) 393-7911

Québec
320 Rue Abraham-Martin
☎(418) 525-3000

Smoking is forbidden on almost all lines and pets are not allowed. Generally children five years old or younger travel for free and people aged 60 or over are eligible for discounts.

By Car

An excellent system of highways and expressways makes Ottawa easy to reach from many points in Ontario and Québec.

From Toronto, follow Highway 7, which crosses Peterborough and goes directly to Ottawa. It is also possible to drive along the St. Lawrence, taking Highway 401 to Prescott and, from there, Highway 16 to Ottawa.

From Montréal, take Highway 40 and then the 417, and get off at the Nicholas St. exit to reach the downtown area.

Things to Consider

Driver's License: As a general rule, foreign driver's licenses are valid for six months from your arrival date in Canada.

Winter Driving: Although roads are generally in good condition, the dangers brought on by drastic climatic conditions must be taken into consideration. Roads are often transformed into virtual skating rinks by black ice. Wind is also a factor, causing blowing snow, and reducing visibility to almost nil. All these conditions, which Canadians are used to, require prudent driving. If you plan on driving through remote areas, be sure to bring along a blanket and some supplies should your car break down.

Driving and the Highway Code: There is no priority to the right. Traffic lights at intersections indicate priority to the right. Signs marked "Arrêt" or "Stop" against a red background must always be respected. Come to a complete stop even if there is no apparent danger.

Traffic lights are often located on the opposite side of the intersection, so be careful to stop on the stop line, a white line on the pavement before the intersection.

When a school bus (usually yellow in colour) has stopped and has its signals flashing, you must come to a complete stop, no matter what direction you are travelling in. Failing to stop at the flashing signals is considered a serious offense, and carries a heavy penalty.

Wearing seatbelts in both the front and back seats is compulsory at all times.

In all provinces except for Québec (and therefore Hull), right turns are permitted on red lights as long as there are no cars in the right lane.

The speed limit on highways is 100 km/h. The speed limit on secondary highways is 90 km/h, and 50 km/h in urban areas.

Gas Stations: Because Canada produces its own crude oil, gasoline prices are less expensive than in Europe, around $0.60 a litre. Some gas stations (especially in the downtown areas) might ask for payment in advance as a security measure, especially after 11pm.

Accidents and Emergencies

In case of serious accident, fire or other emergency, you can dial *911*.

If you run into trouble on the highway, pull onto the shoulder of the road and turn the hazard lights on. If you are driving a rental car, contact the rental company as soon as possible. Always file an accident report. If a disagreement arises over who was at fault in an accident, ask for police help.

Car Rentals

Many travel agencies have agreements with the major car rental companies (Avis, Budget, Hertz, etc.) and offer good values; contracts often include added bonuses (reduced ticket prices for shows, for example).

When renting a car, find out if:

The contract includes unlimited kilometres and if the insurance offered provides full coverage (accident, property damage, hospital costs for yourself and passengers, theft).

Practical Information

Car Rental Companies

Avis
449 Gladstone St.
☎ *230-2847*

Discount
161 Laurier Ave. W.
☎ *234-0814*

Budget
☎ *729-6666*

Hertz
881 St. Laurent Blvd.
☎ *746-6683*

Caution:

To rent a car, you must be at least 21 years of age and have had a driver's license for **at least** one year. If you are between 21 and 25, certain companies (for example Avis, Thrifty, Budget) will ask for a $500 deposit, and in some cases they will also charge an extra sum for each day you rent the car. These conditions do not apply for those over 25 years of age.

A credit card is extremely useful for the deposit to avoid tying up large sums of money.

Most rental cars have an automatic transmission, however you can request a car with a manual shift. Child safety seats cost extra.

Getting Around

By Taxi

Taxi Service

Several taxi companies serve the greater National Capital Region and its is always easy to get a cab. However, it is important to know that even though trips between Ottawa and Hull are commonplace, regulations prevent taxis registered in Québec from picking up passengers in Ottawa, and vice versa. So, it's pointless to hail a taxi with a Québec sign in Ottawa (or one with an Ontario sign in Hull).

Public Transportation

The city of Ottawa boasts an efficient public transportation network. Indeed, there is bus service to any destination in the capital's downtown area. Information concerning the various bus lines is readily available by contacting:

OC Transpo
1500 St. Laurent Blvd.
☎ *741-4390*
⊯ *741-7359*
www.octranspo.com

The price for an adult, senior citizen, student or

teenager (over 12 years of age) is $2.25; the fare for children of six to 11 years of age is $1.25; children under six ride for free.

It is also possible to purchase a "Passejour" ($5), which grants unlimited access to all of the capital's public transportation system for the entire day.

Société de Transport de l'Outaouais
☎ *(819) 770-3242*
Serves the city of Hull. Bus tickets cost $2.60.

Hitchhiking

There are two types of hitchhiking: "free" hitchhiking and "organized" hitchhiking with a group called Allo-Stop. "Free" hitchhiking is more common during the summer, and easier to do outside the large city centres, but it is not recommended and is prohibited on highways.

"Organized" hitchhiking, or ridesharing, with **Allo-Stop** (☎*562-8248*) works very well in all seasons. This efficient company pairs drivers who want to share their car for a small payment with passengers needing a ride. A membership card is required and costs

$6 for a passenger and $7 for a driver per year. The driver receives part (approximately 60%) of the fees paid by the passengers. Destinations include virtually everywhere in the province of Québec so you can use this service to get to Hull. Allo-Stop no longer serves Ontario.

Children under five cannot travel with Allo-Stop because of a regulation requiring the use of child safety-seats.

Money and Banking

Exchange

Most banks readily exchange American and European currencies but almost all will charge **commission**. There are, however, exchange offices that do not charge commissions and have longer hours. Just remember to **ask about fees** and to **compare rates**.

Here are a few financial institutions where you can change money:

Royal Bank of Canada
90 Spatks St.
Ottawa
☎*564-4842*

Exchange Rates*

$1 US	=	$1.50 CAN	$1 CAN	=	$0.66 US
$1 Euro	=	$1.39 CAN	$1 CAN	=	0.72 Euro
£1	=	$2.20 CAN	$1 CAN	=	£0.46
$1 Aust	=	$0.82 CAN	$1 CAN	=	$1.22 Aust
$ NZ	=	$0.66 CAN	$1 CAN	=	$1.52 NZ
1 fl	=	$0.63 CAN	$1 CAN	=	1.58 fl
1 SF	=	$0.91 CAN	$1 CAN	=	1.10 SF
10 BF	=	$0.34 CAN	$1 CAN	=	29 BF
1 DM	=	$0.71 CAN	$1 CAN	=	1.41 DM
100 PTA	=	$0.83 CAN	$1 CAN	=	119.65 PTA
1000 ITL	=	$0.72 CAN	$1 CAN	=	1,392 ITL

*Samples only: rates fluctuate.

Currencies International
50 Rideau St.
Bureau 322, Ottawa
☎569-4075

Custom House Currency Exchange
153 Sparks St.
Ottawa
☎234-6005

Traveller's Cheques

Traveller's cheques are accepted in most large stores and hotels, however it is easier and to your advantage to change your cheques at an exchange office. For a better exchange rate buy your traveller's cheques in Canadian dollars before leaving.

Credit Cards

Most major credit cards are accepted at stores, restaurants and hotels. While the main advantage of credit cards is that they allow visitors to avoid carrying large sums of money, using a credit card also makes leaving a deposit for car rental much easier and some cards, gold cards for example, automatically insure you when you rent a car (check with your credit card company to see what coverage it provides). In addition, the exchange rate with a credit card is generally better. The most commonly accepted credit cards

are Visa, MasterCard, and
American Express.

Banks

Banks can be found almost
everywhere and most offer
the standard services to
tourists. Remember to ask
about any commission fees
before beginning any trans-
actions. Most bank branches
have automated teller ma-
chines (ATMs), which gen-
erally accept foreign bank
cards so you can withdraw
directly from your account
at home for a modest fee.
Long-term visitors are permitted to open a bank
account in Canada, pro-
vided they have two pieces
of identification.

Currency

The monetary unit is the
dollar ($), which is divided
into cents (¢). One dol-
lar=100 cents.

Bills come in 5, 10, 20, 50,
100, 500 and 1,000 dollar
denominations, and coins
come in 1 (pennies), 5 (nic-
kels), 10 (dimes) and 25
(quarters) cent pieces, and
in 1 dollar (loonies) and 2
dollar coins (twoonies).

Taxes and Tipping

Taxes

The ticket price on items
usually **does not include
tax**. In Ontario there are
two taxes, the G.S.T or
federal Goods and Services
Tax, of 7%, which is pay-
able throughout Canada,
and Ontario's provincial
sales tax of 8%. (It is 10%
on alcoholic beverages.)
The provincial sales tax in
Québec is 7.5%.

Tax Reimbursements
for Non-Residents

Non-residents can be re-
funded for taxes paid on
their purchases made while
in Canada. To obtain a
refund, it is important to
keep your receipts. A sepa-
rate form for each tax (federal and provincial) must be
filled out to obtain a refund.
Conditions under which
refunds are awarded are
different for the GST and
the PST (Provincial Sales
Tax). For further information, call ☎*800-668-4748* (for
GST).

Practical
Information

In Ontario you can be rembursed for the provincial tax on each purchase over $625.

☎(613) 746-9200

In Québec, you must present your sales receipts in order to be reimbursed for the provincial sales tax.

☎800-567-4692

Tipping

Tipping applies to all table services, that is in restaurants or other places in which customers are served at their tables (fast food service is therefore not included in this category). Tipping is also compulsory in bars, nightclubs and taxis.

Depending on the quality of the service, patrons must give approximately 15% of the bill before tax. Unlike in Europe, the tip is not included in the bill, and clients must calculate the amount themselves and give it to the waitress or waiter; service and tip are one and the same in North America.

Time Difference

Both Ottawa and Hull are in the same time zone (Eastern Time). The time difference is six hours behind continental Europe and five hours behind the United Kingdom. Daylight Savings Time (+ 1 hour) begins the first Sunday in April and ends the last Sunday in October. Furthermore, do not forget that there are several time zones in Canada, for example when it is noon in Ottawa, it is 9am in Vancouver.

Business Hours and Public Holidays

Business Hours

Stores

Generally stores remain open the following hours:

Mon to Fri
10am to 6pm;
Thu and Fri
10am to 9pm;
Sat
9 am or 10am to 5pm;
Sun
noon to 5pm

Well-stocked stores that sell food, sometimes called convenience stores or variety stores, are found throughout Ontario and are open later, sometimes 24 hours a day.

Banks

Banks are open Monday to Friday from 10am to 3pm. Most are open on Thursdays and Fridays, until 6pm or even 8pm. Automated teller machines are widely available and are accessible night and day.

Post Offices

Large post offices are open Monday to Friday from 9am to 5pm. There are also several smaller post offices located in shopping malls, convenience stores, and even pharmacies; these post offices are open much later than the larger ones.

Public Holidays

The following is a list of public holidays in Ontario. Most administrative offices and banks are closed on these days.

New Year's Day and day after
January 1 and 2

Good Friday or Easter Monday

Victoria Day
3rd Monday in May

Fête de la Saint-Jean
St. Jean Baptiste Day (Québec)
June 24

Canada Day
July 1st

Civic holiday (Ontario)
1st Monday in August

Labour Day
1st Monday in September

Thanksgiving
2nd Monday in October

Remembrance Day
November 1
(only banks and federal government services are closed)

Christmas Day
December 25

Climate and Clothing

Ontario has a continental climate, with very defined seasons. In summer the temperature can reach 30°C, while in the winter it can drop to -25°C; snow is common and often very abundant. In spring and fall, the sun is often hidden behind rain clouds.

Winter

December to March is the ideal season for winter-sports enthusiasts (skiing, skating, etc.). Warm clothing is essential during this season (coat, scarf, hat, gloves, wool sweaters and boots). Toronto and the southwestern part of the province generally benefit

Practical Information

from slightly milder conditions than the rest of southern Ontario.

Spring and Fall

Spring is short (end of March to end of May) and is characterized by a general thaw leading to wet and muddy conditions. Fall is often cool. A sweater, scarf, gloves, windbreaker and umbrella will therefore come in handy.

Summer

Summer lasts from the end of May to the end of August and can be very hot. Bring along T-shirts, lightweight shirts and pants, shorts and sunglasses; a sweater or light jacket is a good idea for evenings.

Health

Vaccinations are not necessary for people coming from Europe, the United States, Australia and New Zealand. On the other hand, it is strongly suggested, particularly for medium or long-term stays, that visitors take out health and accident insurance. There are different types available, so it is best to shop around. Bring along all medication, especially prescription medicine. Un-

less otherwise stated, the water is drinkable throughout Ontario.

In the winter, moisturizing lotion and lip balm are useful for people with sensitive skin, since the air in many buildings is very dry.

During the summer, always protect yourself against sunburn. It is often hard to feel your skin getting burned by the sun on windy days. Do not forget to bring sun screen!

Emergencies

The ☎911 emergency number is in operation throughout most of Ontario and Québec. If it does not work dial *0* and tell the operator that this is an emergency.

Insurance

Before leaving, it's a good idea to make inquires about the various types of insurance available. Take the time to shop around and compare the different rates and conditions which may apply.

Health Insurance

This is the most useful kind of insurance for travellers, and should be purchased before your departure. Your insurance plan should be as complete as possible because health care costs add up quickly. When buying insurance, make sure it covers all types of medical costs, such as hospitalization, nursing services and doctor's fees. Make sure your limit is high enough, as these expenses can be costly. A repatriation clause is also vital in case the required care is not available on site. Furthermore, since you may have to pay immediately, check your policy to see what provisions it includes for such situations. To avoid any problems during your vacation, always keep proof of your insurance policy on your person.

Cancellation Insurance

Your travel agent will usually offer you cancellation insurance upon purchase of your airline ticket or vacation package. This insurance allows you to be reimbursed for the ticket or package deal if your trip must be cancelled due to serious illness or death.

Theft Insurance

Most residential insurance policies protect some of your goods from theft, even if the theft occurs in a foreign country. To make a claim, you must fill out a police report. It may not be necessary to take out further insurance, depending on the amount covered by your current home policy. As policies vary considerably, you are advised to check with your insurance company. European visitors should take out baggage insurance.

Telecommunications

The **area code** of Ottawa and its surrounding region is *613*; for Hull and its surroundings it is *819*. Dialling this code is unnecessary if the call is local. For long distance calls, dial 1 for the United States and Canada, followed by the appropriate area code and the subscriber's number.

Phone numbers preceded by *800* or *888* allow you to reach the subscriber without charge if calling from Canada, and often from the US as well.

Practical Information

If you wish to contact an operator, dial **0**.

When calling abroad you can use a local operator and pay local phone rates. First dial **011** then the international country code and then the phone number.

Country Codes

United Kingdom
44
Ireland
353
Australia
61
New Zealand
64
Belgium
32
Switzerland
41
Italy
39
Spain
34
Netherlands
31
Germany
49

For example, to call Belgium, dial 011-32, followed by the area code (Antwerp 3, Brussels 2, Ghent 91, Liège 41) and the subscriber's number. To call Switzerland, dial 011-41, followed by the area code (Bern 31, Geneva 22, Lausanne 21, Zurich 1) and the subscriber's phone number.

Another way to call abroad is by using the direct access numbers below to contact an operator in your home country.

UNITED STATES
AT&T
☎*800-CALL ATT*
MCI
☎*800-888-8000*

British Telecom Direct
☎*800-408-6420*
☎*800-363-4144*

Australia Telstra Direct
☎*800-663-0683*

New Zealand Telecom Direct
☎*800-663-0684*

Public phones are scattered throughout the city, easy to use and most even accept credit cards. Local calls cost $0.25 for unlimited time. For long distance calls, equip yourselves with quarters ($0.25 coins), or purchase a $10, $15 or $20 phone card, on sale at newsstands. Calling a private residence will cost even less. Paying by credit card or with the prepaid "HELLO!" card is also possible, but be advised that calling by such means is considerably more expensive.

Shopping

In most cases prices are fixed and as indicated. Do

not be surprised, however, if you hear someone asking a store clerk if something is on sale.

What to Buy

Compact Discs: CDs are much less expensive than in Europe, however, they may be more expensive than in the United States.

Furs and Leather: Clothes made from animal skins are of very good quality and their prices are relatively low. Approximately 80% of fur items in Canada are made in the "fur area" of Montréal.

Local Arts & Crafts: These consist of paintings, sculptures, woodwork, ceramics, coppered enamel, weaving, etc.

Indigenous Arts & Crafts: There are beautiful native sculptures made from different types of stone that are generally quite expensive. Make sure the sculpture is authentic by asking for a certificate of authenticity issued by the Canadian government. Good quality imitations are widely available and are much less expensive.

Wine, Beer and Alcohol

The legal drinking age is 19. Beer, liquor and wine can only be purchased at the provincially run "Beer Store," "Liquor Store" and "Wine Store," respectively. These places are open quite late, until 10pm during the week and 11pm on Saturdays. Keep in mind that they are all closed on Sundays.

Advice for Smokers

As in the United States, cigarette smoking is considered taboo, and is being prohibited in more and more public places such as in most shopping centres, in buses and in government offices.

Most public places (restaurants, cafés) have smoking and non-smoking sections. Cigarettes are sold in bars, grocery stores, newspaper and magazine shops.

Safety

By taking the normal precautions, there is no need to worry about your personal security. If trouble should arise, remember to dial the emergency telephone number ☎*911* or *0*.

Practical Information

Children

As in the rest of Canada, facilities exist in Ontario that make travelling with children quite easy, whether it be for getting around or when enjoying the sights. Generally children under five travel for free, and those under 12 are eligible for fare reductions. The same applies for various leisure activities and shows. Find out before you purchase tickets. High chairs and children's menus are available in most restaurants, while a few of the larger stores provide a babysitting service while parents shop.

Travellers with Disabilities

Though considerable efforts have been made to make things more accessible to individuals with disabilities, there is still a lot of work to be done. To facilitate choosing your hotel, the ♿ symbol is included in the description of hotels that have special wheelchair access.

Pets

Ontario is generally quite tolerant of pets, which are permitted in all provincial parks as long as they are on a leash, and remember to properly dispose of their litter. Remember that animals are not allowed in grocery stores, restaurants or buses.

General Information

Illegal Drugs: are against the law and not tolerated (even "soft" drugs). Anyone caught with drugs in their possession risks severe consequences.

Electricity: Voltage is 110 volts throughout Canada, the same as in the United States. Electricity plugs have two parallel, flat pins, and adaptors are available here.

Laundromats: are found almost everywhere in urban areas. In most cases, detergent is sold on site. Although change machines are sometimes provided, it is best to bring plenty of quarters (25¢) with you.

Movie Theatres: There are no ushers and therefore no tips.

Museums: Most museums charge admission. Reduced prices are available for people over 60, for children, and for students. Call the museum for further details.

Newspapers: *Ottawa Citizen*; *Le Droit* (French paper); *X Press* (free weekly cultural paper); *Xtra!* (Gay paper).

Pharmacies: In addition to the smaller drug stores, there are large pharmacy chains that sell everything

Weights and Measures

Although the metric system has been in use in Canada for several years, some people continue to use the Imperial system in casual conversation. Here are some equivalents:

Weights
1 pound (lb) = 454 grams (g)
1 kilogram (kg) = 2.2 pounds (lbs)

Linear Measure
1 inch (in) = 2.54 centimetres (cm)
1 foot (ft) = 30 centimetres (cm)
1 mile (mi) = 1.6 kilometres (km)

Land Measure
1 acre = 0.4047 hectare (ha)
1 hectare (ha) = 2.471 acres

Volume Measure
1 U.S. gallon (gal) = 3.79 litres (L)
1 U.S. gallon (gal) = 0.83 imperial gallons

Temperature
To convert °F into °C: subtract 32, divide by 9, multiply by 5
To convert °C into °F: multiply by 9, divide by 5, add 32.

Practical Information

from chocolate to laundry detergent, as well as the more traditional items like cough drops and headache medications.

Religion: Almost all religions are represented.

Restrooms: Public restrooms can be found in most shopping centres.

JOHN BY

The Rideau Canal
is the heart of Ottawa in two ways.

The very foundation of the city was spurred by the construction of the canal, and, geographically, the canal is the dividing line between the eastern part of the city, called Lower Town, and the western part, known as Upper Town. The first tour described in this chapter runs the length of this crucial waterway and presents the main attractions along its shores. The next two tours, Upper Town and Lower Town, reveal the beautiful architectural achievements that transformed Ottawa's image at the turn of the century. The tours "Sandy Hill" and "Along Sussex Drive" explore the city's attractive residential neighbourhoods. Finally, a visit to Canada's national capital would not be complete without a jaunt across the Ottawa River to Hull, Québec, Ottawa's sister city. Time permitting, pleasant excursions outside

the city are possible, two of which are proposed: one to the charming hamlet of Merrickville and the other to Upper Canada Village, a fascinating re-creation of a 19th-century settlement.

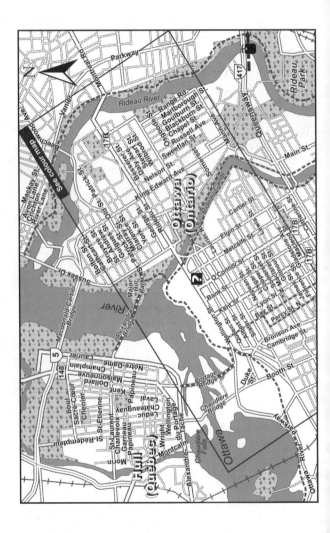

The centre of Canadian politics, Ottawa's Parliament Buildings overlook the Rideau Canal. – *P. Quittemelle*

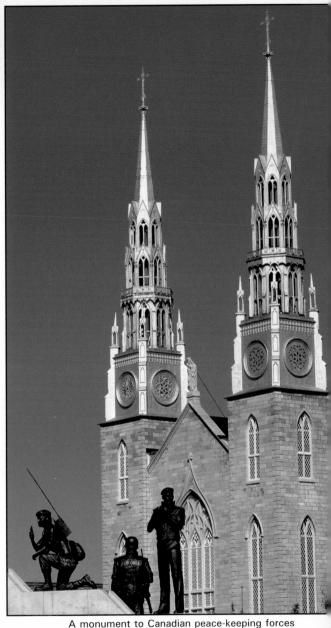

A monument to Canadian peace-keeping forces in front of the Notre Dame Basilica in Ottawa. – *P. Quittemell*

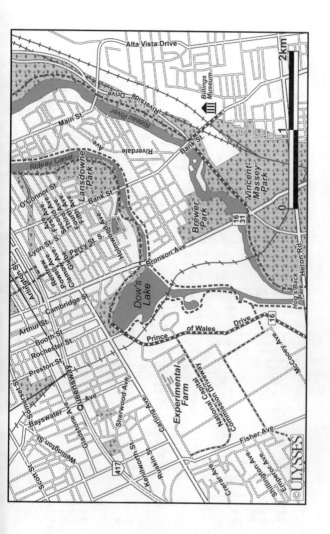

Tour A: the Rideau Canal

Ottawa's existence is in part a result of the British-American War of 1812, in which British authorities realized the extent of the vulnerability of the St. Lawrence River, the vital link between Montreal and the Great Lakes. Once the conflict ended, the British began to devise plans to defend the waterway, and they concluded that a canal linking the south bank of the Ottawa River, at the village of Wrightown, to the city of Kingston would provide the security they desired.

Although it made good use of the Rideau and Cataraqui River networks, the Rideau Canal project required great technological prowess on the part of engineers, as stretches of up to 29km had to be dug. In addition, Colonel By, who was overseeing the work, convinced the authorities to approve a canal not merely 7.6m wide but 15.2m wide, so that it could accommodate all sorts of boats and not just military craft. In sum, the scale of the project was enormous for the day. It took six years to complete, and its price was high in

● ATTRACTIONS

1. Parliament Buildings
2. Langevin Block
3. Infocentre
4. Bank of Montreal
5. Confederation Building
6. Supreme Court of Canada
7. Bank of Canada
8. Memorial Building
9. St. Andrew's Presbyterian Church
10. National Library and Archives of Canada
11. Christ Church Cathedral
12. Currency Museum
13. St. Patrick's Roman Catholic Basilica
14. Bank of Nova Scotia
15. Central Chambers
16. Canadian Museum of Nature

◐ ACCOMMODATIONS

1. Albert at Bay
2. Albert House
3. Capital Hill
4. Carmichael Inn & Spa
5. Cartier Place & Towers
6. Crowne Plaza Hotel
7. Delta Ottawa Hotel & Suites
8. Doral Inn
9. Lord Elgin Hotel
10. Minto Place Suite Hotel
11. Ottawa Marriott
12. Rideau View Inn
13. Hotel Roxborough
14. Sheraton
15. Travelodge
16. Victoria Park Suites

◆ RESTAURANTS

Along the Rideau Canal

1. National Arts Center Café
2. Echo Wine Café
3. Ritz on the Canal

Upper Town

4. Al's Steak and Seafood House
5. Carmello
6. Chez Jean-Pierre
7. Colonnade
8. Connaught
9. Coriander Thai Cuisine
10. D'Arcy McGee
11. Fairouz
12. Fiori's
13. Friday's
14. Hy's Steak House
15. Johnny Farina
16. Le Métro
17. Pancho Villa
18. Ritz
19. Ritz Uptown
20. The Mill Restaurant

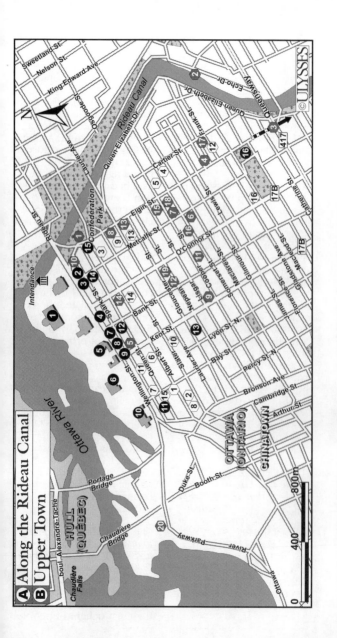

A Along the Rideau Canal
B Upper Town

Intendance

Ottawa River

HULL (QUÉBEC)

Chaudière Falls

Portage Bridge

Chaudière Bridge

boul.-Alexandre-Taché

Parkway

River

Ottawa

Booth-St.

Duke-St.

Bronson-Ave.

Cambridge-St.

Arthur-St.

Percy-St.

Bay-St.

Lyon-St.-N.

Kent-St.

Bank-St.

O'Connor-St.

Metcalfe-St.

Elgin-St.

Queen-Elizabeth-Dr.

Rideau Canal

Confederation Park

Cartier-St.

Frank-St.

Lewis-St.

Gilmour-St.

Nepean-St.

Gloucester-St.

Laurier-Ave.

Slater-St.

Albert-St.

Queen-St.

Sparks-St.

Wellington-St.

Laurier-Ave.

Rideau-St.

Osgoode-St.

King-Edward-Ave.

Nelson-St.

Sweetland-St.

Queen-Elizabeth-Dr.

Echo-Dr.

Queen's River

417

17B

CHINATOWN

OTTAWA (ONTARIO)

800m

400

0

© ULYSSES

N

both financial and human terms: hundreds of people died of malaria and in accidents during the course of the canal's construction. However with its 47 locks and 14 dams, it undeniably represents a formidable technical achievement.

The canal's impressive entrance, created by Scottish mason Thomas McKay, is still visible from the city. It is made up of eight stone locks that permit boats to descend the first 24.4m of the channel. Two mountains overlook the canal, one on either bank. The summit of the eastern hill is now the site of Major's Hill Park (see p 85), but it once bore the stone house of Colonel By, which was destroyed by fire in 1849. The barracks and hospital for the soldiers that built the canal occupied the top of Barrack Hill, on the western shore, until the Parliament Buildings (see p 71) were erected on this site.

The **Intendance** ★ *($2; mid-May to mid-Jun and Sep to mid-Oct, Mon-Thu 8:30am to 4:30pm, Fri-Sun 8:30am to 7:30pm; mid-Jun to Sep, every day 8:30am to 7:30pm; next to the locks)* was built at the foot of Barrack Hill, just next to the locks, in 1827. This stone house is the oldest edifice in the city and it still encloses the Inten-

dance, in which various exhibitions are mounted.

The Rideau Canal does represent a grandiose project in itself, but it was also a turning point in the nation's history, not only because it was at the root of the founding of Ottawa, but also because its construction drew numerous workers to the region, particularly masons. Many of these workers, who were of Scottish origin, settled in the Rideau River Valley and built the stone houses that are so characteristic of this corner of Ontario. The canal also stimulated the development of commerce in Eastern Ontario, bringing a new level of prosperity to local families.

From very early on beautifying the canal was one of the central preoccupations of developers, so starting at the beginning of the 20th century measures were taken to landscape its shores. Its banks were cleared of debris and a panoramic highway was opened on its western shore.

The **Rideau Canal** *(mid-May to mid-June, Mon-Thu 8:30am to 4:30pm, Fri-Sun 8:30am to 7:30pm; mid-Jun to early Sep, every day 8:30am to 7:30pm;* ☎*283-5170 or 800-230-0016)* snakes through Ottawa, to the great delight of people who come for a breath of fresh air right in the heart of the city. In the summer, its banks feature parklands dotted with picnic tables, and there are paths alongside the canal for pedestrians and cyclists. In the winter, once the canal is frozen over, it is transformed into a vast skating rink that crosses the city. There is a small lodge facing the National Arts Centre, where skaters can don their blades and warm up.

The **National Arts Centre** *(53 Elgin St., between Confederation Square and the Rideau Canal, ☎996-7000)* on the west bank of the canal, occupies the former location of Ottawa's 19th-century city hall, which was destroyed by fire.

Aberdeen Pavilion

This centre was built between 1964 and 1967 by Montreal architects Affleck, Desbarats, Dimakopoulos, Lebensol and Sise. Excellent concerts and plays are presented here throughout the year (see p 129, 151), and the advantages of the centre's canal-side location, with its pleasant patios, can be fully appreciated in summertime.

Continue along the canal, either on the Queen Elizabeth Driveway on the west bank or on Colonel By Drive on the east bank.

While on the Queeen Elizabeth Driveway, you'll pass **Lansdowne Park**, a vast public garden where many special events are held throughout the year. It has the added attraction of bordering on the Rideau Canal.

Exploring

Aberdeen Pavilion, the work of architect Moses Edey, is located in the park. Inaugurated in 1898, the pavilion originally served as a place to hold large agricultural fairs and arts and crafts exhibitions. The building's vast interior hall, 94m long and 39m wide, is uninterrupted by supporting columns, creating an impressive exhibition space.

In addition to the exhibition hall, Aberdeen Hall is equally known for having housed the city's first public skating rink. The Senators hockey team (forerunner of the current team), won the Stanley Cup here in 1904. During the 1980s, there were serious thoughts of destroying the hall, as it was being used less and less frequently. However, It was saved at the last moment and renovated in1984.

Dow's Lake is located in an area that was once nothing but swampland. It was artificially created by a dyke and a dam erected during construction of the Rideau Canal. Today this beautiful body of water, situated not too far from downtown Ottawa, is the perfect spot for weekend unwinding: pedal boats, canoes and skates are all available for rent (see p 113), and the lake shore is bordered by a rambling garden that is ideal for picnics and strolls.

Located not far from Dow's Lake, **Commissary Park** is an attractive green space that comes into full bloom in the spring, during the Canadian Tulip Festival, when thousands of tulips opening one after another utterly transform it. The park then becomes a magnet to the many photographers who come to immortalize its vibrantly colourful flowerbeds. Over the course of the year, it is embellished by a variety of other flowers and remains a pleasant urban park.

Tour B: Upper Town

From Bytown's very beginnings, the beautiful west bank of the Rideau Canal was a magnet to the well-to-do English Protestant families who were migrating to the fledgling city. Upper Town, the city's upper-class neighbourhood (if the nascent community could be called a city in those days), became ever more attractive over the years as new houses sprang up to accommodate newly arriving families. The area entered its heyday around the 1860s when Ottawa was chosen as the national capital and the magnificent federal Parliament Buildings were erected on the summit of Barrack Hill. This site belonged to the British Crown at the time and, of course, is still capped by the impressive sight of these government buildings. Within about fifty years, the broad avenues of Upper Town were trimmed with exquisite Victorian buildings as a result of a construction boom in part triggered by the neighbourhood's new prominence.

The half-day tour of this neighbourhood, (not including a tour of the Parliament Buildings themselves), begins at the Parliament Buildings and visits some of the most beautiful architectural sites in the city.

The **Parliament Buildings** ★★★ *(information on activities, ☎239-5000 or 800-465-1867)* truly dominate Ottawa. The summit of the hill is topped by three buildings spread over a 200m² garden.

Centre Block contains the House of Commons and the Senate, the two chambers of the federal government (see p 72). The two other buildings, East Block and West Block, enclose various administrative offices.

In 1857, when Ottawa was designated the capital of United Canada, there was no appropriate edifice in which to accommodate parliament and city authorities realized that it was time to construct a building befitting of the seat of government. A contest was held, and Thomas Fuller and Chilion Jones's plans for a Gothic Revival building won the contract.

Parliament Buildings

Exploring

The deadlines imposed on the designers were very tight and construction began before all of the inevitable kinks in a project of this scale could be worked out. The impressive budget of 250,000 pounds sterling that had been allotted for the project was surpassed barely one year later. Authorities were accused of mismanaging public funds, and work on the building was interrupted. Three years passed before a Royal Commission of Inquiry into the affair recommended that construction resume. In 1866, the first session of Parliament was held in the building, which was still unfinished.

Although construction of Centre Block was riddled with problems, the overall project's final result is justifiably the pride of Ottawa's citizens: three splendid Gothic Revival buildings dominate the horizon of the city, which, up until the erection of the Parliament Buildings, had been a conglomeration of modest wooden houses. At first, Centre Block was comprised of a semi-basement, a ground floor, and only one story. It was topped by a copper mansard roof. At its centre stood Victoria Tower, at a height of 77m, which sheltered the entrance. The House of Commons and the Senate were situated in rooms of equal dimensions in either wing of the building. Construction work was finally completed in 1876.

Just 40 years later, on February 3, 1916, a terrible fire broke out in Centre Block, destroying the rooms of the west wing before spreading to those of the east wing. The magnificent edifice was entirely consumed by flame, with the exception of the **Library of Parliament**, which was spared thanks to the quick wittedness of a clerk who closed the thick iron doors that separated it from the rest of the building. The library, a splendid, 16-sided Gothic Revival building covered by a lantern-shaped roof, may still be visited today. Its interior is richly decorated in white-pine woodwork and comprises a large reading room lit by lancet windows on each of its sides and small alcoves that enclose part of the library collection. Its centre is occupied by a white-marble statue of Queen Victoria that was sculpted by Marshall Wood in 1871.

Reconstruction of Centre Block began some time later and lasted nine years. The architects, John A. Pearson and J. Omer Marchand, designed the new building to be consistent with the East and West

Blocks, opting once again for the Gothic Revival style and reproducing the aspect of the original main building.

Library of Parliament

Guided tours of Centre Block *(free; late May to early Sep, Mon-Fri 9am to 7:40pm, Sat and Sun 9am to 4:40pm; Sep to May, every day 9am to 3:40pm)* visit the

Financial reasons figured in the decision to construct the new building in a style similar to that of its predecessor with like materials. As well, the size of the building had to be reduced, but it was later expanded.

Its facade is pared by the 90m high Peace Tower which encloses, among other features, a carillon of 53 bells. Nothing, however, was omitted in the decoration of the interior of this splendid building, which incorporates particularly magnificent sculptures and woodwork.

interior of the building, including the west wing where visitors are treated to an up-close look at the House of Commons, in which members of parliament elected through universal suffrage hold debates and adopt federal laws. This vast, rectangular, green-toned room is decorated in white pine, limestone and stained-glass windows depicting the floral emblems of the provinces and territories of Canada.

In the east wing of the building, these guided tours pause at the large room that houses the Senate, the Upper Chamber of the federal

Exploring

administration, whose government-appointed members are responsible for studying and approving laws adopted by the House of Commons. This distinctive room is set apart by carpeting and red armchairs, a coffered ceiling adorned with gold maple leaves and two magnificent and imposing bronze chandeliers.

In addition to these two rooms, the guided tours visit the Library of Parliament as well as the Peace Tower, where you can see the white-marble Memorial Chamber.

Beautiful views of the Ottawa river can be had from the **Summer Pavilion** on the grounds of Centre Block, behind the building on the west side.

Since the earliest days of its construction, Centre Block has been flanked on either side by East Block and West Block, the work of Thomas Stent and Augustus Laver. **East Block** *(Jul to Sep, every day 10am to 5:30pm)*, a beautiful composition of asymmetrical elevations, is made of cut stone in shades that range from cream to ochre and is embellished by towers, chimneys, pinnacles, lancet windows, gargoyles and various sculptures. Originally, it was built to house the Canadian civil service; now it encloses the offices of senators and members of Parliament. A guided tour is offered and highlights four rooms that have been restored to their 19th-century appearances. The Office of the Governor General and the Chamber of the Privy Council are also located here. **West Block** is used exclusively for the offices of Members of Parliament and is not open to the public.

Parliament is also the scene of numerous events, notably the **changing of the guard**, which takes place every day from late June to late August at 10am, when you can see soldiers parading in their ceremonial garb. A sound and light show, **Reflections of Canada: A Symphony of Sound and Light** *(free admission; mid-May to early Sep, ☎239-5000 or 800-465-1867)*, presents the history of Canada.

On the vast lawn graced with beautiful flowers stretching in front of the parliament buildings, is the Centennial Flame, inaugurated in 1967 to commemorate the 100th anniversary of Canadian confederation.

In addition to the Centennial Flame, which stands right in the centre of Parliament Hill, there are several statues commemorating outstanding figures in Cana-

The First Industrial Wave: Victoria Island and the Area Surrounding Chaudière Falls

The first industries were set up along the Ottawa River, on Victoria Island and along the Chaudière Falls. This area developed quite naturally, since the Ottawa River was the main communication route and the sole source of energy at the time.

Development started slowly in 1802, with the construction of a sawmill and a mill on the east side of the falls, in response to the needs of the fledgling community of Wrightstown, founded two years earlier (today's Hull). In 1826, with the founding of Bytown (Ottawa) and the start of excavations for the Rideau Canal, demand grew to the extent that several industries developed near the Rideau Falls and on Victoria Island. Development progressed steadily, so that by the end of the 19th century this industrial sector contained more than 30 buildings.

Many of these buildings are now in ruins. However, a few are still in use, such as two stone power stations which were constructed in 1891 and 1900, respectively. You can also still see the Willson Sawmill, the Carbide Mill, the steam power station of the Ottawa Electric Railway Company and the Thomson-Perkins Mill. This latter, built in 1842, is the oldest mill in the region and now houses a restaurant (see p 129).

Exploring

dian history found around the Parliament Building. A walk in the gardens here offers an occasion to learn more about notables like Sir Wilfrid Laurier, Sir John A. Macdonald, Sir George-Étienne Cartier and Lester B. Pearson. You can also arrange to hire a guide (ask at the "Info-tent," located near the West Building).

When the Parliament Buildings were erected, Wellington Street gained in status, and gradually beautiful buildings sprouted up along its sides, each rivalling the others in elegance. Among the Second Empire buildings that were erected during this period (this style was very much in fashion in the capital at the end of the 19th century) **Langevin Block** *(facing the Parliament Buildings, Wellington St.)* may still be admired, standing on the spot opposite the Parliament Buildings that it has occupied since 1889. Also designed by Thomas Fuller but with a more sober look than that of the Parliament, this building was destined to house government offices. Since 1976, it has been the site of the Prime Minister's Office.

The large bay windows of the Ottawa tourist information centre, the **Capital Infocentre** *(90 Wellington St., ☎239-5000 or 800-465-1867, www.capcan.ca)*, are located

two steps away from Langevin Block. A stop here provides a wealth of additional information on accommodations and restaurants in the city, as well as a hotel reservation service.

Stylish Wellington Street has been transformed over the years by new buildings that did not adhere to the Gothic Revival paradigm. At the turn of the 1920s, a branch of the **Bank of Montreal** designed by Ernest I. Barott was unveiled. Its pure Art Deco style is in keeping with the architectural trend of the era for the nation's financial institutions. The stone building has a very simple cubic shape, three sides of which are ornamented with cornices and sculpted with pilasters. The interior is one of the building's crowning glories—it consists of an expansive hall, entirely devoid of columns; rather, it is instead elegantly surmounted by a coffered ceiling.

Ottawa's aesthetic face began to take shape at the beginning of the 20th century, as government buildings were erected to meet the needs of a growing bureaucracy, most of these buildings exhibit the Gothic Revival and Château styles, as the Public Works Department adopted a mandate that endorsed these styles.

Wellington Street was the result of the infatuation with this type of architecture and was embellished with cut-stone buildings that feature pointed roofs, turrets, balconies and dormers. The **Confederation Building** ★, for example, was built next to West Block in about 1928. In the shape of an "L," with an asymmetrical entrance surmounted by a turret with a pointed roof, this building was one of the first projects to combine both of the architectural styles of the day.

Continuing along Wellington Street, another Canadian institution comes into view: the **Supreme Court of Canada** ★ *(May to Aug, Mon-Fri 9am to 12pm and 1pm to 5pm; Sep to Apr, reservations only; corner of Wellington St. and Kent St., ☎995-5361)*. This Art Deco building was conceived by architect Ernest Cormier, who began its construction in 1939. Only one modification was brought to its original plans, which called for a flat roof.

The Public Works Department, which still favoured the Château style, required that the roof be altered to give it its current appearance (or it may have been requested by Prime Minister Mackenzie King). The tremendous interior space created by this peaked roof is now occupied by the court's library.

Facing the Supreme Court stands the **Bank of Canada**. Its austere-looking light-grey granite facade is a geometric composition minimally enhanced by six pilasters and a coat of arms. A few of its elements were inspired by Greek temples, notably a bronze door engraved with a Greek coin and two urns, symbolizing one of the bank's functions, "to keep the wealth." The original architects had foreseen the extension of this beautiful building in their design; 40 years later a 12-story tower was adjoined to the original building.

Exploring

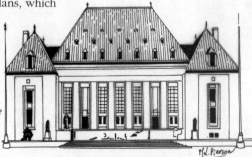

Supreme Court

The Supreme Court

The Supreme Court was created by the Constitutional Act of 1867, but did not really play the role of final appeal court until 1949. Up until then, this function was held by the judiciary committee of the Privy Council in London, a situation that posed complex juridical problems. Despite the fact that Canadian law is inspired by British traditions, there are important distinctions between the two systems. The same building houses the Federal Court of Canada, whose mandate is to settle disputes arising from federal laws.

In 1828, a first stone church was built on land donated to the Presbyterian community by Nicolas Sparks. It rapidly proved too small to house the congregation, so in the 1870s, Montreal architect William Tutin Thomas was commissioned to erect the larger **St. Andrew's Presbyterian Church** *(82 Kent St.)*. Thomas wanted his building to have a colossal appearance and achieved this effect by adding a particularly high spire, one that is actually taller than its supporting tower.

The two edifices that make up the **Memorial Building**, located at the corner of Bank Street, are a more recent interpretation of the Château style, which was in vogue until after the Second World War.

At the end of Wellington Street stand the buildings of the **National Library and Archives of Canada** *(395 Wellington St., ☎992-9359)*, which contain an impressive collection of documents dealing with Canada, as well as Canadian publications. Temporary exhibitions are presented here.

The section of Queen Street between Bay and Bronson is worth a short detour down Bay Street to see its beautiful turn-of-the-century homes.

Three magnificent Queen Anne houses stand at numbers 406-408 and 410. Covered in red brick and ornamented with gables, stained-glass windows and balconies, they are a good indication of what the streets of the city might have looked like at the turn of the century.

Across from St. Andrew's, **Christ Church Cathedral ★** *(439 Queen St.)* is a Gothic Revival building in cut stone that dominates this part of the city. A first church was built on this site in 1833, but it was soon enlarged (in 1840) by adding transepts. With the passing years, it required further expansion, so in 1872, architect King Arnoldi was commissioned to design a new church. However, his original plan had to be revised for economy's sake, and the choir of the new church was reduced. In 1896, Bishop Charles Hamilton made this the seat of the Anglican Church in Ottawa. Christ Church then grew in importance, to the extent that in 1932 it became necessary to... expand the choir! Today, the beautiful interior of this imposing cathedral is still striking, with its gilded sandstone, white marble columns, stained-glass windows and choir.

Queen Street offers little else of interest. A series of high-rises sprouted up in the years around 1965, when the law that proscribed buildings taller than the Parliament was revoked. Businessman Jean Campeau took advantage of this relaxation of restrictions to erect **Place de Ville**, a tall black monolith. Following this lead, many office towers were built in this part of the city. As these are of no particular charm, you can now backtrack to Sparks Street.

The considerable changes that Ottawa underwent in the second half of the 19th century had repercussions on the development of its commercial arteries. From the town's very beginnings, two sections of it have vied for the status of business centre: the surroundings of the Byward Market, in Lower Town, and **Sparks Street**, in Upper Town. Great effort was expended by local residents and shopkeepers to embellish Sparks Street and, thanks to them, this elegant road of five- and six-storey buildings was one of the very first to be paved with asphalt, to have streetcar service and to be illuminated by street lamps. In those days it was known as the "Broadway" of Ottawa. Its commercial role never ebbed, and today it offers a beautiful pedestrian mall between Kent and Elgin streets that is especially pleasant in the summertime when its concentration of pretty shops attracts crowds of patrons and browsers.

Exploring

The first stop on Sparks Street is a visit to the **Currency Museum** ★ *(free admission; May to early Sep, Mon-Sat 10:30am to 7pm, Sun 1pm to 5pm; Sep to Apr closed Mon)*, which is located inside the Bank of Canada, by the rear entrance. The exhibition is spread over eight rooms and retraces the history of the creation of currency. The first room deals with the original objects that served as trading tender: natives used wampum "belts" adorned with shell beads. From there the exhibition traces the evolution of the coin from China, where it had its earliest use, to Florence, where coins were made out of precious metals for the first time (the florin). Rooms three through six cover the development of Canadian currency from the exchange of glassware for beaver pelts, to French colonists' use of playing cards as bills of exchange while they waited money to arrive from France, to the creation of Canadian paper currency. Numismatists will be interested in room eight, which displays a beautiful collection of antique coins and bills. Finally, there is a short educational film about the role of the Bank of Canada.

If you have a little extra time, make a detour down Kent Street to Nepean Street to see **Saint Patrick's Roman Catholic Basilica** ★ *(281 Nepean St.)*, which serves the oldest English-speaking Catholic parish in Ottawa. This long stone building surmounted by a bell tower was finished in 1875. Inside, you can admire its beautiful Gothic Revival interior adorned with stained-glass windows and a Casavant organ.

Backtrack to and continue along Sparks Street.

At number 118 is another branch of a large Canadian bank, the **Bank of Nova Scotia** ★. Erected in 1923-24, this Art Deco building is complemented by a beautiful facade supported by four Doric columns. Above the columns, the building culminates with a frieze of motifs representing prosperity and Canadian history.

Continue to Elgin Street.

The **Central Chambers Building** ★, at the corner of Elgin and Queen, is a good example of the late 19th-century architecture of commercial buildings. Professionals, particularly lawyers, rented office space here, launching the trend that made this neighbourhood so popular. The building was renovated in the early 1980s in a project that preserved its magnificent oblique facade of huge windows, the last row of which, on the fifth floor, is gabled. The ground floor is still occupied by shops.

Bordered by the Rideau Canal and Elgin and Laurier streets in the heart of the capital, a large public garden, **Confederation Park**, hums with activity all year-round. In summer, it is known for the many artists who perform here during the Ottawa International Jazz Festival. It is also a centre of activity in winter, since many of the events of the famous Bal de Neige take place here.

Either continue along Elgin Street—explore its pretty shops or take a break at one of its many restaurants—or, for a longer tour, turn right on McLoed Street to visit the Canadian Nature Museum.

The **Canadian Museum of Nature** ★ *($5; mid-Oct to Apr, Tue-Sun 10am to 5pm, Thu to 8pm; May to mid-Oct, every day 9:30am to 5pm, Thu to 8pm; corner of McLoed St. and Metcalfe St.,* ☎*566-4700)*, in a huge, three-storey building, houses many small exhibitions on various facets of nature. Myriad themes, including geology, the formation of the planet, animals of prehistoric Canada, mammals and birds indigenous to Canada, and the fantastic world of insects and of vegetable life, are presented in an interesting manner.

Tour C: Lower Town

In the early days of Bytown, the poorly irrigated land on the east bank of the canal was unappealing to newcomers. Irrigation work was carried out in 1827, making it more attractive, and it was gradually populated, but not by the well-to-do. Labourers looking for affordable housing established themselves here, and French and Irish workers, most of them Catholic, made up the majority in this neighbourhood. Conditions were difficult; skirmishes between the Irish and the French, who were often competing for the same jobs, were frequent; and life in the neighbourhood was not always rosy. Few traces remain of these first difficult years in Lower Town, as the buildings of the era, most of which were made of wood, rarely resisted the wear of the years. A few which remain are scattered about the neighbourhood and mostly reflect the French origins of the area's residents. Left by the wayside in the second half of the 19th century, the neighbourhood was left out of the building boom that overtook Upper Town.

Exploring

Here, there are very few of the Gothic Revival constructions that were so popular in that period. At the beginning of the 20th century, Sussex Drive, which delimits the western edge of the neighbourhood, was embellished by the construction of magnificent Château-style buildings. Then, over the course of this century, other buildings, including the very beautiful National Gallery of Canada, perfected the image of this elegant artery.

Wellington Street spans the canal, becoming Rideau Street on this bank, where it is lined with a multitude of shops that are fun to browse through a spell. The first building on the tour is the unmistakable and imposing **Château Laurier** ★ ★ *(1 Rideau St.)*, on the shore of the Rideau Canal, which has been one of the most prestigious hotels in the city since the day it opened its doors (see p 21).

(see p 21)

The Château Laurier's origins are intrinsically linked to the construction of the cross-Canada Grand Trunk Railroad. Cornelius

Van Horne, then the head of the Canadian Pacific Railway Company, realized that he needed to increase the number of passengers on this track to make it turn a profit so he decided to establish a coast-to-coast chain of prestigious hotels along the route. The first of these establishments to be erected was the Château Frontenac in Québec City, but the nation's capital would not be outdone: about 15 years later the company contracted Bradford Lee Gilbert to design Ottawa's luxury hotel. Gilbert was let go before construction could begin, so architects Ross and MacFarland were hired in 1908 to complete the blueprints. They favoured the Château style, in keeping with the look of the other Canadian Pacific hotels,

Château Laurier

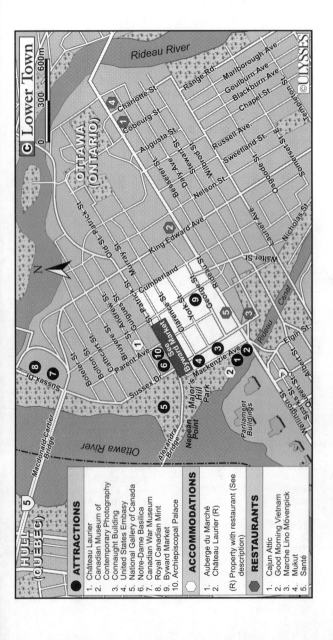

C Lower Town

Rideau River

OTTAWA
(ONTARIO)

Charlotte St.
Cobourg St.
Augusta St.
Béséret Ave.
Daly Ave.
Stewart St.
Nelson St.
Range Rd.
Marlborough Ave.
Goulburn Ave.
Blackburn St.
Chapel St.
Russell Ave.
Sweetland St.

King Edward Ave.

Cumberland
York St.
Clarence
George St.
Rideau St.
Waller St.

St-Patrick
St-Andrew St.
Murray St.
Guigues Ave.
Cathcart St.
Boteler St.
Bruyère St.
Parent Ave.
Sussex Dr.

Sée Market
Byward Market
Major's Hill Park
Nepean Point
Alexandra Bridge

Ottawa River

Macdonald-Cartier Bridge

Parliament Buildings

Rideau Canal

Wellington St.
Sparks St.
Queen St.
Albert St.
Elgin St.
Nicholas Ave.
Laurier Ave.
Osgoode St.
Cumberland St.
Somerset St.

HULL
(QUÉBEC)

0   300   600m

© ULYSSES

● ATTRACTIONS
1. Château Laurier
2. Canadian Museum of Contemporary Photography
3. Connaught Building
4. United States Embassy
5. National Gallery of Canada
6. Notre-Dame Basilica
7. Canadian War Museum
8. Royal Canadian Mint
9. Byward Market
10. Archiepiscopal Palace

○ ACCOMMODATIONS
1. Auberge du Marché
2. Château Laurier (R)

(R) Property with restaurant (See description)

⬢ RESTAURANTS
1. Cajun Attic
2. Good Morning Vietnam
3. Marche Lino Mövenpick
4. Mukut
5. Santé

and built an elegant, romantically alluring hotel with relatively bare stone facades topped by pointed copper roofs, turrets and dormers. No detail was overlooked to make this a top-class hotel, and the interior decoration, which can be admired in the lobby, is absolutely sumptuous. The very first guest to register, in 1912, was none other than Sir Wilfrid Laurier, who had strongly supported the creation of the railroad and in whose honour the hotel was named.

Next to this is the **Canadian Museum of Contemporary Photography** *(free admission; May to Sep, Mon and Tue, Fri and Sun 11am to 5pm, Wed 4pm to 8pm, Thu 11am to 8pm; Sep to Apr, Wed and Fri to Sun 11am to 5pm, Thu 11am to 8pm; 1 Rideau Canal, ☎993-4497)*, with a collection containing more than 158,000 images created from the photographic resources of the National Film Board of Canada.

Continue on Mackenzie Avenue.

Faithful to the architectural tradition that prevailed in the capital at the beginning of the century, the **Connaught Building ★**, erected in 1913-1914, is pure Gothic Revival. Architect David Ewart was inspired by many English buildings of the Tudor era, particularly Hampton Court and Windsor Castle, in the conception of these plans. The building displays crenellated turrets at each end and at its centre.

Sussex Drive is one of the national capital's main arteries and it has been graced with many beautiful buildings since the early 20th century. The United States government selected it as the site for its new **United States Embassy** *(490 Sussex Dr., K1N 1G8, ☎238-5335)*, on the last available lot in this historic area of the city.

A U.S. firm, Skidmore, Owings & Merrill, was chosen to design a modern, functional building that would nevertheless blend in with the architectural landscape of the area. The imposing building, completed in 1999, shows four differently designed facades that are graciously integrated into this historic area of the Canadian capital. What's more, each of the facades had to harmonize with a different setting: the east facade overlooks Lower Town, the west facade faces Parliament and Major's Hill Park, while the north facade opens onto the Peacekeeping Monument, near which many of the various official ceremonies that enliven the city take place.

Major's Hill rises at the mouth of the Rideau Canal, on the east bank. This land which borders the entrance to the canal and the Ottawa River, belonged for a long time to the British Crown, which, when Bytown was founded, had decided to keep it in order to ensure the protection of the canal. The only building erected on its summit was the residence of Colonel By, but it was destroyed by fire in 1849. In 1864, in a project to beautify the city, the land was transformed into a huge park—the city's very first—**Major's Hill Park**. Stretched along the Ottawa River, it remains one of the city's most beautiful green spaces. It envelops **Nepean Point**, which juts into the river and offers a lovely view of the Parliament Buildings. The **Astrolabe Theatre**, where various events are organized in summer, is also within the park confines.

Turn right onto St. Patrick Street.

In 1841, work began on the **Notre-Dame Cathedral–Basilica ★** *(every day 7am to 6pm; 385 Sussex Dr.)*. Its original plan, designed by Jean-François Cannon, was of neoclassical inspiration. However in 1844, after construction was well underway, Fathers Dandurand and Telmon decided to change the style to Gothic Revival. The stone facade with openings for the doors was already completed and was retained, but the vault and windows were then done in Gothic Revival style. Work on the towers, whose spires are 54.5m (178ft) tall, ended in 1858. The church had already become a cathedral as of 1847, and in 1879 it was changed to a basilica.

The church was originally built to serve Catholics in Lower Town, French-speakers as well as the English-speaking Irish. In the choir stall, you will notice the presence of Saint John the Baptist and Saint Patrick. This is the oldest church in the city. Its magnificent choir stall of finely worked wood and statues of the prophets and evangelists by Louis-Philippe Hébert are still in perfect condition.

Behind the Notre-Dame Cathedral–Basilica is the **archiepiscopal palace** *(145 St. Patrick St.)*, whose construction began in 1849. It is the residence for Catholic bishops and, since 1888, for all of the city's Catholic archbishops. Here you can distinguish some of the typical characteristics of French-Canadian buildings such as casement windows, skylights and mansard roofs.

Continue along Sussex Drive.

Exploring

National Gallery of Canada

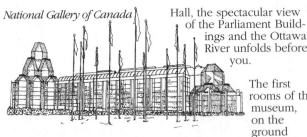

The **National Gallery of Canada** ★★★ *(free admission to the permanent collection; May to Oct, every day 10am to 6pm, Thu 10am to 8pm; Oct to May, Wed to Sun 10am to 5pm, Tue 10am to 8pm; 380 Sussex Dr., ☎990-1985)*, with its collection of 45,000 works of art, 1,200 of which are on display, offers a fabulous trip through the art history of Canada and elsewhere.

Rising above the Ottawa River, this modern glass, granite and concrete building, a masterpiece by architect Moshe Safdie, is easily identified by its harmonious tower, covered with glass triangles, recalling the shape of the parliamentary library visible in the distance.

Once inside, the museum seems to draw you. You'll first walk up the Colonnade, stopping for a minute to contemplate the Boreal Garden outside, inspired by the work of the Group of Seven. Once in the Grand Hall, the spectacular view of the Parliament Buildings and the Ottawa River unfolds before you.

The first rooms of the museum, on the ground floor, are devoted to the works of Canadian and American artists. Fifteen of these rooms trace the evolution of Canadian artistic movements. Some of the finest canvasses from the 19th century are exhibited there, notably *Sister Saint Alphonse* by Antoine Plamondon, recognized as one of the earliest Canadian masterpieces.

You can also see works by Cornelius Krieghoff, an artist of Dutch descent who portrayed the lives of ordinary people in the early days of colonization with great brio.

The following rooms present important works by artists who made their mark in the early 20th century.

Among them, are canvasses by the Ontario painter Tom Thomson (*The Jack Pine*) and by members of the Group of Seven (including *The Red Maple* by A.Y. Jackson), who created unique works with their modern

The Group of Seven

In the early years of the 20th century, some of the great Ontario landscape painters became known by creating genuinely Canadian art. **Tom Thomson**, whose paintings provide a distinctive portrayal of landscapes unique to the Canadian Shield, was an originator of this movement. He died prematurely in 1917 at the age of 40, though his work had an indisputable effect over one of the most notable groups of painters in Ontario, the **Group of Seven**, whose first exhibition was held in Toronto in 1920. These artists, **Franklin Carmichael**, **Lawren S. Harris**, **Frank H. Johnson**, **Arthur Lismer**, **J.E.H. MacDonald**, **Alexander Young Jackson** and **Frederick Varley**, were all landscape painters. Although they worked together closely, each developed his own pictorial language. They were distinguished by their use of bright colours in their portrayal of typical Canadian landscapes. The contribution of these talented artists has greatly influenced Ontario painting.

interpretation of natural scenes from the Canadian Shield. Space is also given to artists who gained renown by creating painting techniques and developing their own particular themes, such as British Columbian artist Emily Carr (*Indian Hut, Queen Charlotte Islands*). You can also contemplate canvasses by great 20th-century Québec painters, notably Alfred Pellan (*On the Beach*), Jean-Paul Riopelle (*Pavane*), Jean-Paul Lemieux (*The Visit*), and Paul-Émile Borduas (*Leeward of the Island*).

The ground floor also includes Inuit art galleries, which are worthy of special attention. With about 160 sculptures and 200 prints, they provide an excellent occasion to admire several masterpieces of Inuit art. Among them, *The Enchanted Owl* by Kenojuak and the beautiful sculpture *Man and Woman Seated with a Child*.

The museum also houses an impressive collection of American and European works. Works of the great masters are presented in chronological order, and in the course of your visit you can contemplate creations by famous painters such as the Pierre-Paul Rubens work *The Entombment*. The rooms containing 19th-century canvasses present several surprises, including *Mercury and Argus* by Turner, *Woman and Umbrella* by Edgar Degas, *Waterloo Bridge: The Sun in the Fog* by Claude Monet, *Forest* by Paul Cézanne, and *Hope I* by Gustav Klimt. The achievements of 20th-century artists are also highlighted; the museum exhibits canvasses including *Nude on Yellow Sofa* by Matisse, *The Small Table* by Picasso, *The Glass of Absinth* by Georges Braque, *Number 29* by Jackson Pollock, and *In the Line of Fire* by Barnett Newman. The collection of American art includes several lithographies by Roy Lichtenstein and Andy Warhol.

The string of rooms on the ground floor surrounds a very unique gallery that houses an under-appreciated work: the beautiful interior of the **Chapelle du Couvent Notre-Dame-du-Sacré-Coeur**, designed by Georges Bouillon in 1887-1888. When the convent was demolished in 1972, the structure of the chapel was taken apart piece by piece and preserved. A few years later, a room was specially laid out in the National Gallery to accommodate it. Its splendid choir and its wooden, fan-shaped vaults and cast-iron columns may still be admired here.

Museum lovers can continue along Sussex Drive to the Canadian War Museum and the Royal Canadian Mint.

The entrance to the **Canadian War Museum** ★ *($4; May to mid-Oct, every day 9:30am to 5pm, Thu to 8pm; mid-Oct to Apr, closed Mon; 330 Sussex Dr., ☎776-8600)* is impossible to miss, what with a tank sitting on the lawn in front of it. The museum was laid out in a beautiful building designed at the beginning of the century by David Ewart to house the National Archives. The exhibitions are spread over three storeys and retrace the history of the Canadian Army from its very first battles in the early days of colonization to its participation in the great world events that have marked the 20th century. Weapons, uniforms and medals of the French military, from the very earliest stages of colonization, and of the British army, which came next, are displayed on the ground floor. These various objects, are not only interesting in and of themselves, but are also used to relate some of the major events of the colonial wars. On the second floor, the Canadian army's involvement in the WW II is recounted through short films, models, weap-

ons of all sorts, uniforms and other objects. Finally, on the top storey, there is an exhibition that highlights the role of peacekeepers.

Just next door to the Canadian War Museum is the building that houses the **Royal Canadian Mint ★** *($2; early Sep to late May, every day 9am to 5pm; late May to early Sep Mon-Fri 9am to 8:30pm, Sat and Sun 9am to 5:30pm; 320 Sussex Dr., ☎993-8990)*, whose plans were conceived by Ewart in 1905-1908. Common Canadian coins were once struck here, but today the mint produces only silver, gold and platinum collector's pieces. The entire process

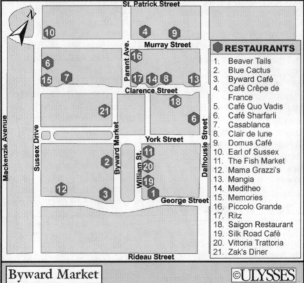

RESTAURANTS

1. Beaver Tails
2. Blue Cactus
3. Byward Café
4. Café Crêpe de France
5. Café Quo Vadis
6. Café Sharfarli
7. Casablanca
8. Clair de lune
9. Domus Café
10. Earl of Sussex
11. The Fish Market
12. Mama Grazzi's
13. Mangia
14. Meditheo
15. Memories
16. Piccolo Grande
17. Ritz
18. Saigon Restaurant
19. Silk Road Café
20. Vittoria Trattoria
21. Zak's Diner

may be seen here: the selection and cutting of precious metals, the striking of the coins and the quality control procedure. It is best to visit during the week when it is possible to see the coins being made through large bay windows; tours are offered on the weekend, but in the absence of workers the whole process has to be imagined.

Backtrack to Clarence Street and turn left. Turn right onto Byward and proceed to the Byward Market.

One of Ottawa's liveliest places, the **Byward Market** ★★ *(around York and George sts.)* is a pleasant open-air market where various merchants assemble to sell fruits, vegetables, flowers and all sorts of other treasures and knick-knacks. All around, and on the neighbouring streets, there are many shops, restaurants, bars and cafés, some with pretty outdoor terraces. On fine summer days, the area is at its most lively, with relaxed crowds of people out for a stroll and shoppers seeking out special ingredients.

Tour D: Sandy Hill

In Bytown's earliest days, the city developed in two sections, Upper Town and Lower Town. The designa-tion of Ottawa as Canada's national capital led to profound changes as the city underwent major growth: myriad buildings went up to meet the needs of new-comers. Around the 1870s, a new class began to emerge, made up of bu-reaucrats and federal government representatives, all of whom would have to live in the capital. These people earned comfortable incomes for their efforts and moved into a new neigh-bourhood called Sandy Hill, between Rideau and Mann streets, on land that until then had been the undi-vided property of Louis Besserer. This area of the city, comprised of beautiful homes and lush gardens, remains one of Ottawa's most attractive.

Take Rideau Street to King Edward Avenue and turn right.

At the corner of Daly Street and King Edward Avenue there is a Georgian house of cut stone that dates from 1844. Built well before the area became fashionable, this home belonged to Louis Besserer, who owned all of the land that would become the neighbourhood known first as the St. George Ward and later as Sandy Hill.

St. Alban the Martyr, a cut-stone church that dates

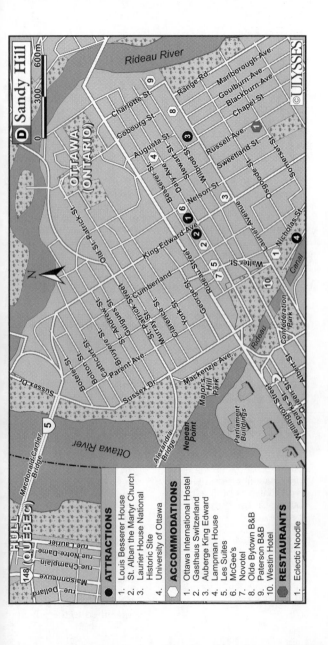

D Sandy Hill

0 300 600m

Rideau River

Marlborough Ave.
Goulburn Ave.
Blackburn Ave.
Chapel St.

OTTAWA
(ONTARIO)

Charlotte St.
Cobourg St.
Augusta St.
Range Rd.
Russell Ave.
Sweetland St.
Osgoode St.
Somerset St.

Nelson St.
King Edward Ave.

Cumberland St.
Waller St.
Nicholas St.

Canal

Old St-Patrick St.
St-Andrew St.
Guigues St.
Bruyère St.
St-Patrick St.
Murray St.
Clarence St.
York St.

Cathcart St.
Bolton St.
Cobourg St.

Besserer St.
Daly Ave.
Wilbrod St.
Stewart St.

Rideau Street

George Street

Laurier Avenue

Confederation
Park

Rideau

Ottawa River
Macdonald-Cartier
Bridge

HULL
(QUEBEC)

rue Laurier
rue Notre-Dame
rue Champlain
Maisonneuve
rue Dollard

148

Sussex Dr.
Beausoleil Dr.

Alexandra
Bridge

Nepean
Point

Mackenzie Ave.
Sussex Dr.
Parent Ave.

Major's Hill
Park

Wellington Street
Sparks Street

Parliament
Buildings

N

© ULYSSES

ATTRACTIONS
1. Louis Besserer House
2. St. Alban the Martyr Church
3. Laurier House National
   Historic Site
4. University of Ottawa

ACCOMMODATIONS
1. Ottawa International Hostel
2. Gasthaus Switzerland
3. Auberge King Edward
4. Lampman House
5. Les Suites
6. McGee's
7. Novotel
8. Olde Bytown B&B
9. Paterson B&B
10. Westin Hotel

RESTAURANTS
1. Eclectic Noodle

from 1867, is just across King Edward Avenue. The choir and transepts were added in 1877. Construction of this Gothic Revival church was begun by Fuller, the architect credited with the Central Block of the Parliament, and finished by King Arnoldi. Today it is the oldest still-standing Protestant church in the city.

Continue east on Daly Street, a thoroughfare that is especially interesting to architecture buffs because it is lined with buildings reflecting a variety of styles, including beautiful upper-class residences side-by-side with working-class homes.

The red-brick McFarlane row houses that stand at number 201 constitute one of the area's earliest developments (1868).

Among the pretty houses on the street that date from the last century, one that stands out is Winterholme House (at 309-311), a stone house with a wood-shingle roof that was built as a residence for the queen's printer.

Continuing along Daly Street there are more beautiful examples of the architecture of the late 19th century. Turn right on Charlotte Street, then left on Wilbrod Street.

Paterson House, designed by architect J. W. H. Watts between 1901 and 1903, sits at 500 Wilbrod Street. This gorgeous Queen Anne house has not lost any of its charm with age; in 1992 it was impeccably renovated and converted into a bed and breakfast (see p 121).

Strathcona Park sprawls along the Rideau River at the end of Charlotte Street, providing a beautiful green space and an ideal spot for a short rest, where you can contemplate the lovely Ottawa River.

Turn right on Laurier Avenue.

Laurier House ★ *($2.25; Apr to Sep, Tue-Sat 9am to 5pm, Sun 2pm to 5pm; Oct to Mar, Tue-Sat 10am to 5pm, Sun 2pm to 5pm; 335 Laurier Ave. E., ☎692-2581)*, a delightful residence built in 1878, belonged to Sir Wilfrid Laurier. He was elected Prime Minister of Canada in 1896, and that year his party, the Liberal Party of Canada, offered him this house. Laurier was the first French-speaker to become Canadian prime minister, a post he held until 1911; he lived in this house until his death in 1919. Later, Lady Laurier gave it to William Lyon Mackenzie King, who succeeded her husband as Liberal leader. When King died in 1950, the house was bequeathed to the government as part of Canada's heritage. Visiting it today, you can explore several rooms decorated according to King's tastes and a few others decorated with the Laurier family's furniture.

Ottawa University, previously known as Ottawa College, was originally run by a religious order and served the Catholic communities of Ottawa. Now the university is a renowned educational institution. Its campus is bordered by Laurier Avenue, Nicholas Street and King Edward Avenue.

The end of Laurier Avenue abuts the Rideau Canal.

The Ottawa Congress Centre, located on the shore of the canal, hosts various events throughout the year.

Tour E: Along Sussex Drive

Past the Royal Canadian Mint, Sussex Drive runs along the eastern bank of the Ottawa River to a posh section of the city. This tour is best explored by car or by bicycle since the attractions are rather spread out.

The first stop is **Earnscliffe**, a superb Gothic Revival residence overlooking the Ottawa River that dates from 1856-1857. It was originally home to the family of John MacKinnon, son-in-law of Thomas McKay, who designed the entrance to the Rideau Canal. A few years after MacKinnon's death in 1870,

Earnscliffe

Prime Minister John A. Macdonald was a tenant here. He bought the house about 10 years later and lived out the rest of his years in it. Today Earnscliffe is home to the British High Commission.

At Green Island the Rideau River empties into the Ottawa River in two pretty waterfalls that form a curtain (hence the river's name; *rideau* is French for "curtain"). Take a moment to stop at the belvedere at the top of the falls; it offers a magnificent **view ★** of the

Exploring

river and of the city in the distance.

Ottawa City Hall ★ *(111 Sussex Dr.)* stands on Green Island, and its modern look was the pride of the city in 1958 when it was inaugurated. Over the years the city administration outgrew this stone, aluminum and glass building, but since they wanted to preserve this attractive structure, they decided to expand, rather than replace it. Moshe Safdie, the architect of the National Gallery of Canada (see p 86), was commissioned to oversee the work.

Also situated on Green Island, the **Canada and the World Pavilion** *(☎239-5000)* is scheduled to open in 2001. This learning centre will be dedicated to distinguished Canadians who have gained world-wide acclaim in sports and culture, as well as in international development. Interactive displays will feature the accomplishments of famous Canadians like Lucille Teasdale and Céline Dion, along with the discoveries of Canadian scientists.

A series of magnificent homes appears next, but number 24 should catch your eye. It is an immense stone house surrounded by a beautiful garden—the **Official Residence of the Prime Minister of Canada**. Built in 1867 for businessman Joseph Currier, it became the home of Canadian prime ministers in 1949. For obvious reasons it is not open to the public.

Not far from 24 Sussex Drive another splendid residence crops up, surrounded by a vast, pleasant garden that covers 40ha: **Rideau Hall** ★★ *(free admission; schedule varies; 1 Sussex Dr., ☎998-7113)*. This is the official residence of Canada's governor general, the representative of the Queen of England, Elizabeth II. It is a sumptuous Regency-style home that was built in 1838 for Thomas McKay, the designer of the entrance to the Rideau Canal (see p 68) In 1865, the government rented the building to accommodate the governor general of the day, Lord Monck, and then bought the property in 1868. Since then, many modifications have been made to the original building, which has been in continual use as an official residence.

Take a few minutes to enjoy the sumptuous garden, where you can linger about Guided tours are offered during the summer of the five rooms open to the public.

By strolling the streets surrounding Rideau Hall, you will no doubt be impressed

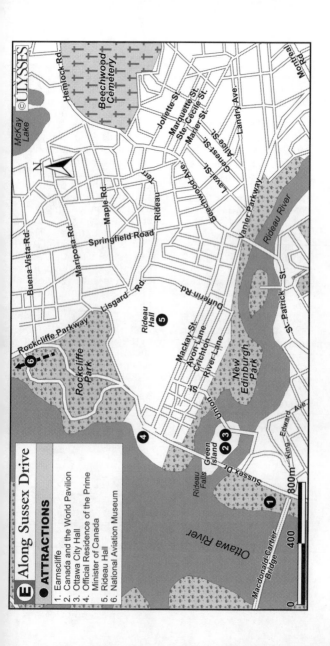

E Along Sussex Drive

● ATTRACTIONS

1. Earnscliffe
2. Canada and the World Pavilion
3. Ottawa City Hall
4. Official Residence of the Prime Minister of Canada
5. Rideau Hall
6. National Aviation Museum

©ULYSSES

by the area's beautiful houses, some of which have been converted into embassies.

Facing Rideau Hall is a lovely green space, **Rockliffe Park**, with lookouts offering fine views of Hull and the Gatineau River.

Past the park, Sussex Drive becomes Rockliffe Drive.

Visitors will immediately be intrigued upon entering the **National Aviation Museum ★ ★ ★** *($6; May to Sep, every day 9am to 5pm, Thu to 9pm; Sep to Apr, Tue-Sun 10am to 5pm, Thu to 9pm; Rockliffe Airport,* ☎*993-2010)* by the unique atmosphere of this huge, wonderfully laid-out building. The fascinating exhibition housed here and culled from the museum's beautiful collection of airplanes thoroughly brings to light the dazzling, rapid-fire evolution of an industry that is just 100 years old.

Eight themes are developed here: the era of pioneers, the First World War, bush piloting, airlines, the British Commonwealth training plan, the Second World War, air and sea forces, and the era of jet planes.

Among the 45 planes displayed in the interior of the museum (the museum's collection includes some other planes in addition to those on exhibit—a total of 118 in all), some are particularly captivating. An exhibit features models of wood and canvas planes that were the first ever to take to the air, and a short film relates the exploits of the first brave pilots to ride these flying engines. The Curtiss HS-2L and the sturdy Beaver are used to illustrate the importance of commercial flying in the exploration of Canada's immense territory.

Planes that became famous in the Second World War, such as the Avro Lancaster bomber, the Hawker Hurricane fighter and the Messerschmitt, a German-designed jet, are highlighted. Finally, a few jets are displayed, including the Lockheed F-104A Starfighter.

The appeal of this museum, aside from the airplanes, lies in the great story of aviation that it retells through reconstructions and consistently clear ex-

The magnificent glass tower of the National Gallery of Canada, a masterpiece by architect Moshe Safdie. – *Neil Valois*

Architectural treasures of the National Capital Region: the Canadian Parliament in Ottawa and the Canadian Museum of Civilization in Hull. – 7

planations of both technical and historical aspects. Interactive exhibitions—particularly "Full Flight," which uses games to explain the basic principals of aerodynamics—along with films and demonstrations, including the very popular "Lighter than Air," aim to familiarize young people and the young-at-heart with the aeronautical world. An audio tour may be rented ($2).

Tour F: Other Attractions

Ottawa has a few other sights worth visiting that, although not far, are located outside the city centre and not within the confines of any tour described above.

From downtown take Rideau Street, which becomes Montreal Road past Cummings Bridge, to St. Laurent Boulevard, which leads to the National Museum of Science and Technology.

The **National Museum of Science and Technology** ★★ *($6; May to Sep, every day 9am to 5pm; Sep to Apr, Tue-Sun 9am to 5pm; 1867 St. Laurent Blvd., ☎991-3044)* offers a great opportunity to enter the world of science and technology—a universe that may seem too complex at first glance to some. The

appeal of this museum is not based on any particular exhibition but rather on its panoply of interactive presentations on various subjects. For example, computer science is tackled in an exhibition entitled "Connexions": about 500 computers are displayed, illustrating the extraordinary technological leaps and bounds that the field has made in just 50 years. Another exhibition, "Love, Leisure and Laundry," recounts the evolution of the multitude of little tools used in our daily lives—like lamps, toilets and iceboxes—that have greatly contributed to our improved standard of living. Other fascinating topics are also dealt with, such as transportation and printing. Through games, explanatory panels and models of all sorts, visitors to the museum gain a better understanding of how the world works and have fun at the same time.

From downtown take Queen Elizabeth Drive, then Bank Street to Riverside Drive, then Pleasant Park Road to the intersection of Cabot Street.

The Billings family were among the first colonists to settle in Bytown. In 1827-1828 a beautiful neoclassical home was built for them; it has survived all these years and now houses

Exploring

Three Ottawa Neighbourhoods

Somerset Street is a long thoroughfare lined with charming shops and restaurants that crosses the southern part of Upper Town from east to west. The first little nexus of businesses is located in the vicinity of Bank Street. Going west, strollers will discover yet another facet of the capital: **Chinatown**. Although it is not as large as those of Montréal or Toronto, Ottawa's Chinatown does cover a few blocks between Bronson and Booth. It has a flurry of storefronts filled with a thousand and one Chinese products, shops fragranced by Oriental spices and restaurants with menus featuring Dim Sum and Cantonese specialties.

East of Bank Street, Somerset intersects Preston Avenue, a north-south artery that fostered the development of another very pleasant ethnic neighbourhood, **Little Italy**. Although to some this neighbourhood might seem less exotic than Chinatown, it does conceal a few gratifying finds, including fine grocery stores and family restaurants that serve incomparable cuisine.

Finally, the **Glebe**, which extends out from Bank Street south of Queensway, is a lively, stylish neighbourhood of chic boutiques and fine restaurants. This peaceful residential area is ideal for sunny-day strolls., where you can take your time wandering about, and feast your eyes on the neighbourhood's many beautiful houses.

the **Billings Estate Museum**
*($2.50; May to Oct, Tue-Sun
noon to 5pm; 2100 Cabot St.,
☎247-4830)*. Furniture, pho-
tographs and various curios
are exhibited, illustrating
daily life in the early days
of the city, and the helpful
guides will make your visit
all the more enjoyable. A
large garden of flowers and
trees surrounds the building.

ent breeds of cattle. Also,
there are tonnes of facts
about the day-to-day work-
ings of a farm and the animals that are raised. Outside, there are pens where
you can watch cows and
sheep frolicking. A variety
of guided activities allow
both young and old to fa-
miliarize themselves with
life on a farm. Can't fail to
please!

Billings Estate Museum

*From downtown take Queen
Elizabeth Drive, which becomes Prince of Wales Drive.*

Children will love visiting
the **Agricultural
Museum** ★★*($5; every day
9am to 5pm; Prince of Wales
Dr., ☎991-3044)* where
they'll discover an actual
experimental farm with
sheds housing all kinds of
farm animals (cows, pigs,
sheep, goats and rabbits)
that they can observe at
their leisure. You can see
calves that are barely a few
days old, or learn how to
differentiate between differ-

Carleton University *(Colonel By
Dr., www.carleton.ca)* has
figured prominently among
Ottawa's institutions since
1942. Originally, its found-
ers wanted to create a non-
denominational institution
in response to the establishment of the University of
Ottawa, run by clergy. Over
the course of the years,
Carleton University has
carved a place among
Canada's respected seats of
learning. The vast campus
has several buildings.
Among these, St. Patrick's
Building houses the **Carleton
University Art Gallery** *(☎520-*

Exploring

2120) where paintings by both contemporary and historical Canadian artists are exhibited, as well as diverse art objects from around the world.

Cold War fears led many western countries, including Canada, to adopt a variety of measures against a potential nuclear attack. To this aim, a bomb shelter was built outside the national capital to protect the country's main political leaders. The days of the Cold War are long gone, and people can now visit this unique shelter: the **Diefenbunker, Canada's Cold War Museum** *($12; reservations required; every day 10am to 3pm; 3911 Carp Rd., ☎839-0007 or 800-409-1965).* Tour guides will fill you in on the history of the era and explain how the Diefenbunker came to be built. To get here, take Highway 417 west to the Carp exit. Plan on an approximately 35min drive from Ottawa.

Tour G: Hull, Québec

The Du Portage Bridge crosses the Ottawa River over Victoria Island, leading from Ottawa to Hull. The area at the foot of the bridge on the Ottawa side

of the river was once known as Lebreton Flats, and an industrial district developed there in proximity to the sawmills. Until the decline of the lumber industry in the 20th century, piles of wood cluttered the banks of the river, but today the only traces of this era that remain are the defunct mills on Victoria Island.

Although the road leading into Hull is named after an important post-war town planner, the city is certainly not a model of enlightened urban development. It's architecture is very unlike that of Ottawa, just across the river. The town was founded in 1800 by American Loyalist Philemon Wright who was involved in agriculture and the exploitation of the Ottawa Valley's rich virgin forests. In 1850, Hull became an important wood-processing centre. For many generations the Eddy Company, which is based in the area, has been supplying matches to the entire world.

The modest wood-frame houses that line the streets of Hull are nicknamed "matchboxes" because they once housed many employees of the Eddy match factory, and because they have had more than their fair share of fires. In fact, Hull has burned so many times throughout its history that few of the town's historic buildings remain. The former town hall and beautiful Catholic church burned down in 1971 and 1972, respectively. Ottawa has the reputation of being a quiet city, while Hull is considered more of a fun town, essentially because Québec laws are more lenient.

Turn left onto Rue Papineau. The parking lot of the Musée Canadien des Civilisations is at the end of this street.

tween 1983 and 1989. Hull became the site of the magnificent Musée Canadien des Civilisations, dedicated to the history of Canada's various cultural groups. If there is one museum that must be seen in Canada it is this one. Douglas Cardinal of Alberta drew up the plans for the museum's two striking curved buildings, one housing the administrative offices and restoration laboratories, and the other the museum's collections.

Canadian Museum of Civilization

The **Canadian Museum of Civilization** ★★★ *($5, free admission on Sun 9am to noon; May to Sep every day 9am to 6pm, Thu to 9pm; Jul to Apr Fri to 9pm; Oct to Apr every day 9am to 5pm, Thu to 9pm; 100 Rue Laurier, ☎819-776-7000).* Many parks and museums were established along this section of the Québec-Ontario border as part of a large redevelopment program in the National Capital Region be-

Their undulating design brings to mind rock formations of the Canadian Shield, shaped by wind and glaciers. There is a beautiful view of Ottawa River and Parliament Hill from the grounds behind the museum.

The **Grande Gallerie** (Great Hall) houses the most extensive collection of native totem poles in the world.

Exploring

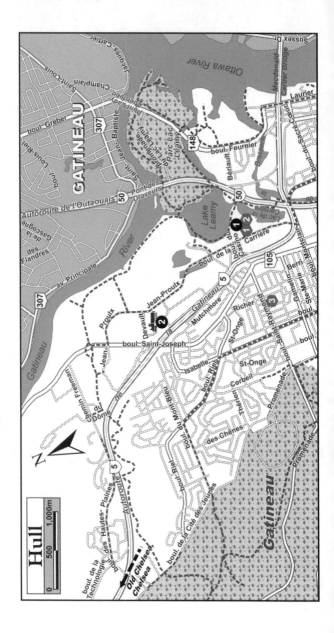

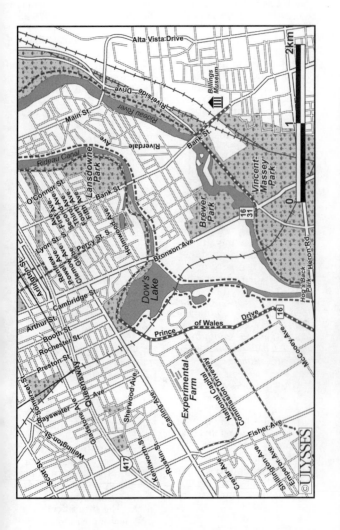

Another collection brilliantly recreates different periods in Canadian history, from the arrival of the Vikings around AD 1000 to life in rural Ontario in the 19th century and French Acadia in the 17th century. Contemporary native art, as well as popular arts and traditional crafts are also on display. In the Musée des Enfants (Children's Museum), young visitors choose a theme before being led through an extraordinary adventure. Screening rooms are equipped with OMNIMAX technology, a new system developed by the creators of the large-screen IMAX. Most of the movies shown here deal with Canadian geography.

Take Maisonneuve Boulevard, then Highway 5 heading north until the Boulevard du Casino exit. Follow Rue Saint-Raymond, which becomes Boulevard du Casino.

If you continue your tour by taking Rue Laurier heading south, you will come across the building that houses the **Maison du Citoyen** (*25 Rue Laurier, ☎819-595-7175*), which is Hull's city hall. In addition to a library and conference rooms, there is also a small art gallery.

Continue south on Rue Laurier. At Rue Montcalm, turn right.

The mission of the **Écomusée de Hull** (*$5; Apr to Oct 10am to 6pm, Nov to Mar 10am to 4pm; Rue Montcalm, ☎819-595-7790*) is to make people more aware of ecological issues. To achieve this goal, it presents various exhibits on themes such as the origin of the solar system and the evolution of planet earth. This institution, however, goes beyond tracing the origins of life on earth, because it is also home to an insectarium with no less than 4,000 different species of insects. Finally, you can also take a look at a small exhibit on the industrial history of the city.

Take Highway 50, then Highway 5 north to the Boulevard du Casino exit. Then take Rue Saint-Raymond, which becomes Boulevard du Casino.

The **Casino de Hull** ★★ (*11am to 3am; 1 Boulevard du Casino, ☎819-772-2100 or 800-665-2274*) has an impressive location between two lakes; Leamy Lake, in the park of the same name, and Lac de la Carrière, which is in the basin of an old limestone quarry. The theme of water is omnipresent all around the superb building, inaugurated in 1996. The magnificent walkway leading to the main entrance is dotted with towering fountains, and the harbour has 20 slips for

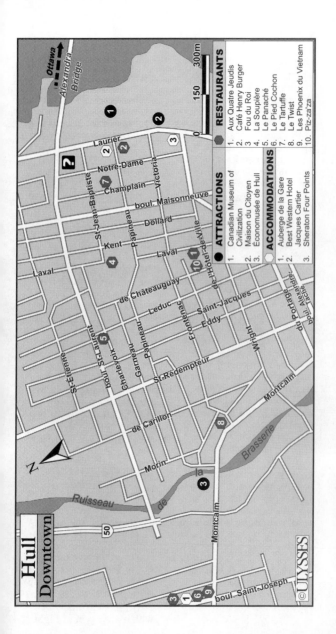

Hull
Downtown

Ottawa
Alexandra Bridge

300m
150
0

Laurier
Notre-Dame
Champlain
boul. Maisonneuve
Dollard
Kent
Laval
de Châteauguay
Leduc
Saint-Jacques
Eddy
St-Rédempteur
de Carillon
Morin
Ruisseau
50
boul. Saint-Joseph
Montcalm
Brasserie
de la
Wright
Frontenac
Papineau
Garneau
Charlevoix
boul. St-Laurent
St-Étienne
St-Jean-Baptiste
Papineau
Victoria
de l'Hôtel-de-Ville
du Portage
boul. Alexandre-Taché

N

© ULYSSES

boaters. The gambling area, which is 2,741m² in size, includes 1,300 slot machines and 58 playing tables spread around a simulated tropical forest. The opening of the casino also marked the first annual fireworks festival, **Fireworks at the Casino** (☎819-771-FEUX or 800-771-FEUX), which takes place every year in August. There are some excellent restaurants on the premises, including Baccara (see p 145), as well as two bars. The casino opened a heliport in 1997.

Continue driving south of the Ottawa River. Take Boulevard de la Carrière to Rue Deveault.

Imagine contemplating the magnificent landscape of Gatineau Park while comfortably seated aboard a steam engine dating back to 1907: **the Hull-Chelsea-Wakefield Steam Train** ★ *($26; late May to late Oct, departures Sat-Thu 1:30pm, Fri 10am; 165 Rue Deveault, ☎819-778-7246, ≠819-778-5007)*. gives you a chance to behold some beautiful natural sites. This half-day excursion takes you to Wakefield, a charming little English town, where you have two hours to explore and shop. If you're interested in the trip but don't want to take the train both ways, you can cross Gatineau Park on bicycle and return

by train. Packages including a meal are also available.

Gatineau Park ★ *(6$; visitor centre is located in Chelsea, also accessible via Boulevard Taché in Hull; ☎827-2020)* is not far from downtown Hull. The 35,000ha park was founded during the Depression in 1934 in order to protect the forests from people looking for firewood. It is traversed by a 34km-long road dotted with panoramic lookout points, including the **Belvédère Champlain**, which offer superb views of the lakes, rivers and hills of the region. Outdoor activities can be enjoyed here throughout the year. Hiking and mountain biking trails are open during the summer. There are many lakes in the park, including Meech Lake, which was also the name of a Canadian constitutional agreement drawn up nearby but never ratified. Watersports such as windsurfing, canoeing and swimming are also very popular, and the park rents small boats and camp sites. **Lusk Cave**, formed some 12,500 years ago by water flowing from melting glaciers can be explored. During the winter, approximately 190km of cross-country skiing trails are maintained *(approx. $7 per day)*. **Camp Fortune** *(☎827-1717)* has 19 downhill-ski runs, 14 of which are open at night.

The cost is $24 during the day and $20 at night.

The **Mackenzie-King Estate** ★★ ($6 for parking; mid-May to mid-Jun, Wed-Sun 11am to 5pm; mid-Jun to mid-Oct, 11am to 5pm; Rue Barnes in Kingsmere, Gatineau Park, ☎613-239-5000 and 827-2020).

William Lyon Mackenzie King was prime minister of Canada from 1921 to 1930, and again from 1935 to 1948. His love of art and horticulture rivalled his interest in politics and he was always happy to get away to his summer residence near Kingsmere Lake, which today is part of Gatineau Park. The estate consists of two houses (one of which is now a charming tea room), a landscaped garden and follies, false ruins that were popular at the time. However, unlike most follies, which were designed to imitate ruins, those on the Mackenzie-King estate are authentic building fragments. For the most part, they were taken from the original Canadian House of Parliament, destroyed by fire in 1916, and from Westminister Palace, damaged by German bombs in 1941.

Tour H: Merrickville

From Ottawa, take Colonel By Drive South, which runs along the Rideau Canal for some distance. At the end of this road, turn left on Brookfield Road then right on Riverside Drive, which becomes Route 19, and follow it until Kemptville. From here, take Route 43 to Merrickville.

A surprising number of splendid stone buildings line the streets of this small village. Dating back to the 19th century, they bear witness to the former wealth of this hamlet. In 1793, William Mirick began constructing mills next to the waterfalls located here on the Rideau River, and this led to the village's prosperity. During the 19th century, the town's development kept pace with the building of the Rideau Canal. The advent of the railways, however, curtailed Merrickville's prosperity, when the town was by-passed by railway builders. One positive repercussion of this decline, however, is that the village was spared from modernization, and its distinct character seems frozen in time.

Walking alongside the Rideau Canal, the first building you come to is the **Merrickville Public Library** ★ (Main St.), built in the 1890s by William Pearson. This elegant brick building has a gable and a veranda. It was Pearson's daughter Mary who bequeathed this su-

Exploring

perb dwelling to the town to house its library.

In front, the **Sam Jakes Inn** is the former residence of Samuel Jakes, who had it built in 1861. It has now been converted into a stylish and comfortable inn.

Continue along Main Street until Saint Lawrence Street.

The **Blockhouse** *($1; mid-May to mid-Oct, every day;* ☎692-2581) is the biggest military building erected along the Rideau Canal, and its function was to protect the boats using this waterway. It could accommodate up to 50 soldiers, and today houses a small museum.

Turn left on Saint Lawrence Street.

At the edge of the Rideau River is the Merrickville **industrial zone ★**, with the ruins of the mills that once assured the village's prosperity. Among these buildings, the oldest of them built in 1793 by William Mirick, you will see a sawmill, a weaving mill, a flour mill and an oat processing mill. Not far from this area, on Mill Street, is William Mirick's last residence.

Return along Street Lawrence Street.

Saint Lawrence Street is lined with a cluster of shops, each more charming than the last, where you can linger for hours in front of the tempting display windows. For those who wish to explore the other treasures in this delightful village, a small brochure entitled *Merrickville Walking Tour* is also available.

Tour I: Upper Canada Village

Morrisburg would be just another little town if it weren't for the proximity of Upper Canada Village. This remarkable tourist attraction consists of houses from eight little villages that were flooded when the water level of the river was raised during the construction of the St. Lawrence Seaway. The houses were moved to Crysler Farm Battlefield Park, where they now make up a fascinating historical reproduction of a 19th-century community. The park also has a small monument commemorating the Canadian victory over American troops in the War of 1812.

With 35 buildings, **Upper Canada Village ★★★** *($9.50; May to Oct, every day 9:30am to 5pm; Crysler Farm Battlefield Park, 11km east of Morrisburg, on Rte. 2,* ☎613-543-3704) is an outstanding reconstruction of the type of village found in this part of Canada back in the 1860s. The place has a remarkably authentic feel about it, and you will be continually surprised by the extraordinary attention to detail that went into building it. A sawmill, a general store, a farm, a doctor's house... nothing is missing in this village that you can explore on foot or by horse-drawn cart. To top off this almost idyllic tableau, the "villagers" are costumed guides able to answer all your questions. Their carefully designed outfits reflect both their trade and social class. You can spend several hours exploring Upper Canada Village and watching the various inhabitants go about their daily activities, such as running the sawmill, working on the farm and using the flour mill.

Outdoors

Since the earliest days of the city, the creation of green spaces was a priority for city leaders, who, over the years, proceeded to lay out vast, beautiful parks and gardens.

Whether you are looking for an urban park such as Major's Hill or Rockliffe, or untouched natural spaces like Gatineau Park, the Ottawa-Hull region has a bit of everything to please nature lovers and outdoor enthusiasts. All of these natural attractions are located either in or near the city. Hiking, cycling and cross-country skiing are among the sports that are easily practised in the national capital region.

Outdoor Activities

Hiking

An activity accessible to just about everyone, hiking outings, from short walks to more challenging excursions in the forest, are possible in various locations in the city and its surroundings. You can stroll along the Rideau Canal or the Ottawa River for a few hours, on pleasant walkways laid out along these waterways; if you enjoy longer excursions, the path along the canal runs all the way to Kingston. You can also opt for a nature trek in Gatineau Park.

A beautiful promenade is maintained along the Rideau Canal that is very easy to follow. This path actually constitutes the first metres of the 400km-long **Rideau Trail**, which runs through the forests and undulating landscapes of Eastern Ontario, along the edge of the Canadian Shield from Ottawa to Kingston. Some parts of the trail feature parallel paths. For a map of the Rideau Trail contact the **Rideau Trail**

Association *(P.O. Box 14, Kingston, ON, K7L 4V6)*.

Gatineau Park *(☎827-2020)* offers a great number of hiking trails, over 125km in all, and just as many opportunities to discover this park's striking beauty. You can explore Lac Pink, a beautiful but polluted lake (you can't swim in it), on a 1.4km trail. If you prefer splendid panoramic views, choose Mont-King, a 2.5km-long trail that leads you to the summit and some gorgeous views of the Ottawa River Valley. And finally, if you have a bit more time and are interested in a fascinating excursion, the Lusk Cave trail is 10.5km long and leads to 12,500-year-old marble cave.

Cycling

The Ottawa region is crisscrossed by no fewer than 150km of pathways that are very pleasant for meandering on foot or by bicycle. Whether you opt for an outing along the Rideau Canal, on the Rockliffe promenade or along the Ottawa River, you will benefit from pleasant landscapes, from peace and quiet and, above all, from trails that are very well laid out for cycling. On Sunday mornings from late May to early September, cyclists are in seventh heaven, as these routes are closed to automobile traffic. Maps of Ottawa's bicycle and walking paths are available at the capital Infocentre.

Bicycle Rental in Ottawa

Cyco's
5 Hawthorne Ave.
☎567-8180

Dow's Lake Pavilion
☎232-1001

Velocation
Château Laurier
☎241-4140

Cruises

As soon as the fine weather arrives, cruises operate along the waterways surrounding Ottawa. You can take part, seeing the city from a different angle and drifting quietly on the waves. Several companies offer such excursions, notably:

Ottawa Riverboat
$14
30 Murray St., Ottawa, Ont., K1N 5M4
☎562-4888

Perhaps you have noticed the *Lady Dive*, a surprising red vehicle sporting large picture windows, which drives through the streets of Ottawa before setting sail on the Ottawa River. This unique "amphibus" tour gives visitors an opportunity to see the city's major attractions and to admire its skyline as well.

Amphibus Lady Dive Tours
May to Jun and Sep to Oct, every day 10am to 4pm; Jul to Aug, every day 9am to 9pm
☎852-1132

Canoeing and Kayaking

On beautiful sunny days, you don't have to leave the city to do some canoeing or kayaking; you can rent these at the **Dow's Lake Pavilion** *(1001 Queen Elizabeth Dr.,* ☎232-1001*)*.

You my prefer to be surrounded by nature, in which case you should contact **Trailhead** *(1960 Scott St.,* ☎722-4229*)*, an outfit located in Ottawa that organizes canoe trips in Gatineau Park. These excursions vary in duration from one to several days. Accompanied by guides, your

Outdoors

outing will be both safe and enjoyable, and you are sure to take in some terrific scenery.

Skating

Imagine lacing on a pair of skates and gliding uninterrupted for over 8km of ice. Every winter, as soon as the **Rideau Canal** has frozen over, in late December or early January, it is transformed into a vast skating rink, one of the longest in the world. The ice surface is cleared and maintained for the pleasure of skaters of all ages. A heated cabin is at the disposal of visitors just a few steps from the National Arts Centre which allows skaters to lace up away from the cold.

Dow's Lake also possesses a heated lodge in which winter sports enthusiasts can don their skates, warm up and have a bite to eat.

Ice Conditions: ☎*239-5234*.

Cross-Country Skiing

In winter, when there's a thick layer of snow, **Gatineau Park** maintains no less than 200km of cross-country ski trails. These trails, 47 in all, are sure to delight skiers of all levels.

Accommodations

A wide choice of accommodation to fit every budget is available in Ottawa and Hull.

Most places are very comfortable and offer a number of extra services. Prices vary according to the type of accommodation, but the quality-to-price ratio is generally good; remember, however, to add the 7% GST (federal Goods and Services Tax) and the provincial sales tax of 5% in Ontario and 7.5% in Québec. The Goods and Services Tax is refundable for non-residents in certain cases (see p 53). A credit card will make reserving a room much easier, since in many cases payment for the first night is required.

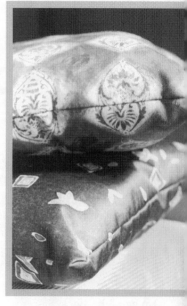

Many hotels and inns offer considerable discounts to employees of corporations or members of automobile clubs (CAA, AAA). Be sure to ask about corporate and other discounts as they are often very easy to obtain. You'll also find many coupons in the free brochures available at various travel associations. Often, if the hotel is not booked, special arrangements can be made for you for no extra charge. For example, you can ask for a room with a better view or a corner room for

Ulysses's Favourites

For history buffs:
Château Laurier, p 124

For Victorian charm:
Auberge King Edward, p 123
Olde Bytown Bed and Breakfast, p 122
Carmichael Inn & Spa, p 121

For elegant decor:
Paterson B&B, p 123

For businesspeople:
Westin, p 124

the same price as a standard one.

The symbols found in parentheses following the name of the establishment will help you make your choice. Take note, however, that these may not apply to each room in the hotel. You will find the list of symbols and their explanations at the beginning of this book. Since most accommodations offer a private bathroom with each room, we have only mentioned those with shared bathrooms.

Hotels

Hotel rooms abound, and range from modest to luxurious. Most hotel rooms come equipped with a private bathroom. There are several internationally reputed hotels in Ontario, including some spectacular establishments that are part of the Canadian Pacific chain.

Inns

Often set up in beautiful historic houses, inns offer quality lodging. These types of establishments are plentiful, and are more charming and usually more picturesque than hotels. Many are furnished with beautiful period pieces. Breakfast is often included.

Upper Town

See map, p 67.

Right in the city, on the Lebreton flats, travellers will find a small, friendly **campground** (*$7.50/person, free for children under 12; Jun to early Sep; tents only;* ☎*236-1251*) which can easily be reached by a bicycle path as well as by car or bus. It is run by the National Capital Commission and has 200 places, with toilets, showers and picnic tables. Reservations are not accepted.

Doral Inn
$69
K
486 Albert St., K1R 5B5
☎*230-8055 or 800-263-6725*
⇌*237-9660*
www.doralottawa.com
Visitors can stay in close proximity to the Parliament Buildings on Albert Street, which changes character in this part of Ottawa – the shops and the hubbub of downtown giving way to a quiet residential district (some may even fault it for being virtually devoid of shops). This area lays claim to two charming inns. The Doral Inn, the first of these is set up in a lovely Victorian house and contains about forty rooms. Just off the hall are two small lounges appointed with secondhand furniture, giving them an antiquated look

that will appeal to some. The rooms are simply furnished and offer decent comfort for the price. All are equipped with private bathrooms and some also have kitchenettes. Rooms can be rented for the day, the week, or the month.

Albert House
$80 bkfst incl.
478 Albert St., K1R 5B5
☎*236-4479*
⇌*237-9079*
Next door, the Albert house is also located in an appealing residence. There are only 17 rooms, giving it a pleasant family atmosphere. Each of the rooms is perfectly maintained and decorated with care.

Rideau View Inn
$70 sb
$85 pb
177 Frank St., K2P 0X4
☎*236-9309 or 888-658-3564*
⇌*237-6842*
www.bbcanada.com/91.html
The Rideau View Inn is set in a large Edwardian house furnished in period style. Facing a small public park with tennis courts, this nonsmoking residence offers seven rooms, two of them with private bath and one with a sitting room. Guests can also use the lounge with its fireplace and television, as well as a terrace on the top floor.

Lord Elgin Hotel
$80-$100
ℜ, &
100 Elgin St., K1P 5K8
☎*235-3333 or 800-267-4298*
≈235-3223
www.lordelginhotel.ca

The Lord Elgin Hotel is among those timeless Ottawa institutions. Very few pieces of furniture, however, have managed to conserve any traces of its past. The sole exception is the lobby which still has a pretty centre light and an antique mobile hanging from the ceiling. The rooms, for their part, are large and decorated with modern furnishings that may fail to lend the charm of yesteryear, but make for a pleasant stay nonetheless.

Capital Hill
$90
ℜ
88 Albert St., K1P 5E9
☎*235-1413 or 800-463-7705*
≈235-6047
www.capitalhill.com

In the vicinity of Parliament Hill, the stark and old-fashioned building housing the Capital Hill hotel offers well-kept, relatively large and comfortable rooms, with rather commonplace decors. This hotel is a decent alternative for nights when other hotels in the city are full.

Hotel Roxborough
$95 bkfst incl.
ℜ
123 Metcalfe St., K1P 5L9
☎*237-9300*
≈237-2163

The economy hotel chain Days Inn has taken over a little hotel that occupies a 19th-century building- the Hotel Roxborough. The plainly decorated rooms and aging furniture are not exactly charming, but provide an adequate level of comfort. This hotel benefits from a great location, not far from Elgin Street and the National Arts Centre.

Victoria Park Suites
$100
⌂, K, ☺
377 O'Connor St., K2P 2M2
☎*567-7275*
≈567-1161
www.victoriapark.com

Victoria Park Suites is a good spot to keep in mind if you want to be just a few steps from Parliament Hill with your own kitchenette and an impeccably kept room.

Crowne Plaza Hotel
$109
101 Lyon St., K1R 5T9
☎*237-3600 or 800-567-3600*
≈237-2351

If there is one hotel that has neglected to keep up with the times, it is certainly the Crowne Plaza Hotel. Indeed, it seems that few efforts have been made to win visitors over: the hall is

Accommodations

adorned with a few stunted plastic plants and the imitation marble walls do not succeed in giving the place any soul. Moreover, as if to match the environment, even the welcome is dour. The hotel does have comfortable rooms, however, and offers several excursion packages.

Cartier Place & Towers
$120

≈, △, ☺, K

180 Cooper St.

☎**236-5000 or 800-236-8399**

⇌**238-3842**

www.suitedreams.com

With over 200 rooms each featuring a kitchenette, small living room and balcony, the Cartier Place & Towers is a choice locale for those wishing to spend a few days in the capital. The establishment also offers a fitness centre and a pleasant patio surrounded by a bit of greenery.

Albert at Bay
$125

K, ☺

435 Albert St., K1R 7X4

☎**238-8858 or 800-267-6644**

⇌**238-1433**

www.albertatbay.com

At first glance, the Albert at Bay, a banal building, looks more like a high-rise apartment complex that has seen better days than a hotel. This place is, however, a good choice for practical reasons rather than charm.

Every suite offers a bedroom, a living room, a dining area and a fully equipped kitchenette (microwave oven, coffee-maker). Over and above the comfort of a real apartment, guests also benefit from the perks of a hotel such as a daily cleaning service and a fitness centre.

Delta Ottawa Hotel & Suites
$125

≈, ℜ, △, ☺

361 Queen St., K1R 7S9

☎**238-6000 or 800-268-1133**

⇌**238-2290**

www.deltahotels.com

As you enter the Delta Ottawa Hotel & Suites, you will straightaway notice the extra touches which create a more intimate atmosphere than the typical downtown chain hotel. The glass ceiling allows plenty of light to penetrate the vast lobby. The ficuses add some greenery, while mahogany chairs and a warm fireplace invite guests to cosy up during the winter. The rooms are a good size and furnished with comfortable mahogany pieces. Finally, children will be thrilled with the pool's long waterslide.

Minto Plaza Suite Hotel
$125
K, &, ℜ
433 Laurier Ave. W.
☎*232-2200 or 800-267-3377*
✆*232-6962*
www.mintohotel.com

In the heart of downtown stands the high-rise building housing the Minto hotel. The rooms here are not decorated with any particular originality, but they are perfectly suited to business travellers. Each one has a desk large enough to work at comfortably as well as a small living room and a kitchenette. In the basement, visitors will find a shopping mall and restaurants.

Ottawa Marriott
$125
≈, △, ⊛, ℜ, &
100 Kent St., K1P 5R7
☎*238-1122 or 800-853-8463*
✆*783-4229*
www.radisson.com

Though this concrete high-rise may seem common and somewhat short on charm at first glance, several little details have been added to provide the quality of lodging offered by other big hotels in the city. That translates into a polite welcome and a foyer sufficiently elegant to be inviting. The rooms, though decorated with beige formica furniture, are eminently comfortable. Finally, the fitness centre is very pleasant.

Sheraton
$125
≈, ℜ, △, ⊘, &
150 Albert St., K1P 5G2
☎*238-1500 or 800-489-8333*
✆*238-8497*

While some prefer older establishments filled with antiques and an elegant decor, still others opt for modern styling and the utmost in service. Those who fit into the latter category will appreciate the very modern Sheraton with its conference halls, large rooms with offices, telephones with voice-mail, hair dryers and fitness centre offering a pool, sauna and whirlpool.

Travelodge
$125
⊛, ⊘, K
402 Queen St., K1R 5A7
☎*236-1133 or 800-578-7878*
✆*236-2317*

At the western end of Queen Street stands the Travelodge, an attractive red-brick building whose modern architecture manifests a certain studied elegance. However, its outer appearance belies the character of the rooms within. Though relatively spacious, their decor is somewhat lacking in charm. Moreover, guests are constantly assailed by a succession of garish advertisements placed all over the hotel (elevator, reception), to remind them of the hotel's affiliations. However, this tactic ultimately succeeds only in displaying a lack of class. Fortunately, many little advantages, such as a coffee machines, hair dryers and fax reception at no extra charge, make these minor inconveniences negligible. Some of the rooms have kitchenettes.

Carmichael Inn & Spa
$149- $189 bkfst incl.
ℜ
46 Cartier St., K2P 1J3
☎ *236-4667 or 877-416-2417*
⇆ *563-7529*
www.carmichaelinn.com

Set in an imposing old house, the Carmichael Inn & Spa is part of Ottawa's heritage. This non-smoking establishment has 11 rooms that are decorated with antiques and fitted with queen-size beds.

Lower Town and Sandy Hill

See map on p 83.

Those seeking low-priced accommodations during the summer can rent one of the basic but adequate rooms in the residence halls at both **Ottawa University** *(85 University St., K1N 6N5, ☎562-5771, ⇆562-5157)* and **Carleton University** *(1125 Colonel By Promenade, K1S 5B6, ☎520-5611, ⇆520-3952)*.

Ottawa International Hostel
$18.95 per person
$37 for a room
K, P
75 Nicholas St., K1N 7B9
☎ *235-2595 or 800-663-5777*
⇆ *235-9202*
www.hostellingintl.on.ca

Right next to the Rideau Centre, in the middle of everything, you will see an imposing building that once housed the city's prison. Entirely remodeled, it now houses the Ottawa International Hostel. In addition to dormitories and three rooms, the hostel has a fully-equipped communal kitchen.

L'Auberge du Marché
$69 bkfst incl.
87 Guigues St., K1N 5H8
☎ *241-6610 or 800-465-0079*

Dating from the early 20th century but entirely renovated, L'Auberge du Marché is a charming little house. There are three rooms upstairs and a shared bathroom, as well as a suite on the ground floor with a private bathroom, a full kitchen, and a small lounge with sofa-bed and cable television. Breakfast varies each day, but is always plentiful and refined. Guests have a private entrance allowing them to come and go as they please.

Accommodations

Lampman House
$60- $70 bkfst incl.
sb
369 Daly Ave., K1N 6G8
☎241-3696
⇌789-8360
Those with an appreciation
for old buildings will also
be delighted with the
Lampman House bed and
breakfast, a lovely Geor-
gian-style residence. This
row house, a testament to
the district's early days,
boasts three rooms ele-
gantly decorated with an-
tique furnishings and cu-
rios.

McGee's
68$- 150$
⊛, ≡
185 Daly Ave., K1N 6E8
☎237-6089 or 800-2MCGEES
⇌237-6201
The Sandy Hill district is
sure to charm fans of the
Victorian style. If you count
yourself among them but
do not have the means for
extravagances, the McGee
Inn is a good choice.
Erected in 1886, this red-
brick house has succeeded
in retaining its original cachet. Admittedly, the rooms
are simply decorated, but
they are tasteful nonetheless. Moreover, the place is
well-kept and all the rooms
are air conditioned.

**Olde Bytown Bed and
Breakfast**
$75 bkfst incl.
pb, sb
459 Laurier Ave. E., K1N 6R4
☎565-7939
⇌565-7981
www.midioldebytown.com
Located in a quiet neigh-
bourhood and affording a
superb view of Strathcona
Park, the Olde Bytown Bed
and Breakfast is a choice
place for those who appreciate the ambiance of
turn-of-the-century Victorian
houses. Every room here is
meticulously kept and
graced with beautiful an-
tiques, flowered wallpaper
and old artifacts. There are
seven wonderfully cosy
rooms where guests can
easily pass away the hours
relaxing and daydreaming.

Gasthaus Switzerland
$88- $118
89 Daly Ave., K1N 6E6
☎237-0335 or 888-663-0000
⇌594-3327
The impeccably kept
Gasthaus Switzerland is a
small, unpretentious hotel
whose Swiss-chalet-style
decor may be a little too
colourful for some tastes.
You will have a restful stay,
however, for the owners
are friendly, breakfasts are
plentiful, and the atmo-
sphere is convivial.

Accommodations

Auberge King Edward
$80
525 King Edward Ave., K1N 7N3
☎565-6700 or 800-841-8786
www.bbcanada.com/464.htm

The Auberge King Edward is set up in a very beautiful house dating from the beginning of the century. In keeping with the period of the building, all the rooms are graced with antiques and myriad old curios. This somewhat cluttered decor has undeniable charm and imparts an atmosphere of calm and well-being to the establishment. The inn features two charming living rooms as well as three exceedingly well-kept bedrooms (one with a private bathroom).

Les Suites
$100
≈, ℜ, △, ⊛, ♿, ✠
130 Besserer St., K1N 9M9
☎232-2000 or 800-267-1989
⇌232-1242
www.les-suites.com

If you prefer the comfort of a suite at a reasonable price, Les Suites welcomes you. Just a few steps from the Rideau Centre, you will enjoy a one- or two-bedroom apartment with full kitchen, dining room and lounge. Children under 18 stay free. The hotel also has an indoor pool.

Novotel
$125
ℜ, ≈, △, ⊘
33 Nicholas St., K1N 9M7
☎230-3033 or 800-NOVOTEL
⇌760-4765

With its dark blue foyer trimmed with steel and wood, the Novotel stands apart from the city's Victorian hotels. This modernity is not without refinement, despite the fact that some will describe it as cold. While the rooms are somewhat warmer, their dark colours pleasantly adorn the spacious quarters, all including a rather large bathroom.

Paterson B&B
$135 bkfst incl.
500 Wilbrod St., K1N 6N2
☎565-8996
⇌565-6546

At the very end of Wilbrod Street stands the magnificent stone building housing the Paterson B&B, one of the district's gems. This monumental Queen Anne house was entirely renovated in 1992 by experts who carefully ensured that its treasures of yesteryear were preserved. Its cut-stone façade proudly heralds the splendours awaiting inside. Upon entering you will immediately be captivated by the panelled walls and ceilings, finely-wrought wainscotting, beautiful antique furniture, carpets and a grand wooden staircase leading to the rooms upstairs. The Victorian decor of the four rooms combines antique furnishings, floral prints, and frames and curios of all kinds. The establishment's good taste extends to the private bathrooms, all exceedingly charming and impeccably clean. Some rooms benefit from small boudoirs where guests can watch TV. Breakfast is served in a vast and elegant dining room. A very gracious welcome completes this idyllic scene.

Westin Hotel
$135
≈, ℜ, △, ⊛, ⊘, 占, 🐾
11 Colonel By Dr.
☎560-7000 or 800-937-8461
≈560-7359
www.westin.com

Facing the Rideau Canal, opposite the National Arts Centre and right in the heart of Ottawa's bustle, the Westin Hotel has what may be the most enviable location in Ottawa. This hotel is part of the complex that includes the Rideau Centre shopping mall and the Ottawa Convention Centre. Rooms are very spacious and extremely comfortable, offering magnificent views of the canal. On the premises you will find a very good restaurant, Daly's (excellent atmosphere, interesting and refined cuisine), and even a happening night club. Very

good weekend packages are usually available.

🚣 Château Laurier
$169
≈; △; 占
1 Rideau St., K1N 8S7
☎241-1414 or 800-866-5577
≈562-7030

The opulence and luxury of the Château Laurier, part of the Canadian Pacific hotel chain, will appeal to those who are enthralled by beautiful things. Upon entering the hotel, visitors will be swept away by the decor: wainscotted walls, cornices, bas reliefs and antiques. The lobby itself hints at of the comfort and elegance of the rooms, all stocked with wooden furnishings, plush couches and comfortable beds. Undeniably appealing, the rooms combine a bygone elegance with today's conveniences. Two very good restaurants and a sports centre with a lovely Art Deco swimming pool add to the place's overall splendour.

The Glebe

Blue Spruces Bed & Breakfast
$85 bkfst incl.
187 Glebe Ave., K1S 2C6
☎236-8521 or 888-828-8801
≈231-3730

Located on a quiet street in the pleasant Glebe district, the Blue Spruces Bed & Breakfast is enchanting. This elegant Edwardian house is furnished with 19th-century Victorian and Canadian antiques. The luxury of the decor is rivalled only by that of the bedding. And if that is not enough, the breakfasts and the hospitality of the owner will round out the enchantment. It only welcomes non-smokers.

Outside Ottawa

Those who must stay in the Ottawa region but do not wish to enter the city itself can find accommodations along Highway 417, where three establishments succeed each other: the **Comfort Inn** (*$82; 1252 Michael St., K1J 7T1, ☎744-2900 or 800-424-6423, ≠746-0836),* the **Chimo** (*$115; ⊘, ≈, ℜ; 1199 Joseph Cyr St., K1J 7T4, ☎744-1060 or 800-387-9779, ≠746-0836),* which rivals the other hotels in the city by providing modern sports facilities, and the **Welcome Inn** (*$85; 1220 Michael St., K1J 7T1, ☎748-7800 or 800-387-4381, ≠748-0499).*

Hull

See map, p 105

Auberge de la Gare
$88 bkfst incl.
205 Boulevard St-Joseph, J8Y 3X3
☎*778-8085 or 800-361-6162*
≠*595-2021*
The Auberge de la Gare is a simple, conventional hotel that offers good value for your money. The service is both courteous and friendly, and the rooms are clean and well kept, albeit nondescript.

Sheraton Four Points
$149
ℜ, ≈,
35 Rue Laurier, J8X 4E9
☎*778-6111 or 800-272-6232*
≠*778-8548*
The Hôtel Ramada Plaza is located opposite the Musée des Civilisations. It is a simple-looking building in the typical chain-hotel style, and the rooms are stocked with nondescript, functional furnishings. Renovations will be taking place in 2001.

Best Western Hôtel Jacques-Cartier
$165
≈, ℜ
131 Rue Laurier, J8X 3W3
☎*770-8550 or 800-265-8550*
The small, austere lobby of the Best Western Hôtel Jacques-Cartier is hardly inviting. Decorated with modern furniture, the rooms are neither cozy nor

luxurious, but are nonethe-less comfortable.

Merrickville

Milliste Bed & Breakfast
$68 bfkst incl.
≡
205 Mill St., K0G 1N0
☎269-3627
⇄269-4735

Milliste Bed & Breakfast is a very charming place if you want to relax in a peaceful setting. Situated in an attractive brick house and surrounded by a pretty garden, it is beautifully decorated with antique furniture, curios and paintings that give it an inviting atmosphere. On the main floor, a sitting room and dining room welcome guests. Upstairs, five comfortable, individually decorated rooms also assure a pleasant stay.

Sam Jakes Inn
$112-$150 bkfst incl.
⌂, ⊘,
118 Main St. E., K0G 1N0
☎269-3711 or 800-567-4667
⇄269-3713
www.samjakesinn.com

You might just as easily be swayed in favour of the delightful Sam Jakes Inn, a very well renovated stone building that was constructed in the last century. The rooms are furnished with antiques and decorated with wallpaper. The soft eiderdowns on all the beds are part of the management's efforts to create a cozy environment. The old-fashioned style blends perfectly with the modern comforts. Most of the main floor is occupied by an immense restaurant (see p 146) where delicious meals are prepared. This is a non-smoking establishment.

Restaurants

The city of Ottawa abounds in restaurants of all kinds.

Whether you are partial to steak, roast beef, or fish; to French, Italian, Asian or other specialties, the city's restaurants are sure to fulfil your expectations. A number of them are open for both lunch and dinner; keep in mind, however, that satisfying your hunger after 11pm can prove difficult.

The restaurants described here generally offer a good selection of dishes and sometimes a fixed-price menu consisting of an appetizer, a main course and coffee. Whatever your choice, be advised that in the great majority of cases, prices do not include taxes. You must add 7% federal tax (GST) and 8% Ontario provincial tax (PST) (7.5% in Québec) to your bill, as well as a 15% tip (or more, according to the quality of the service).

Unless otherwise indicated, the prices mentioned in the guide are for a meal for one person, not including taxes, drinks and tip.

$	$10 or less
$$	$10 to $20
$$$	$20 to $30
$$$$	$30 or more

Restaurants by Type of Cuisine

Belgian

Sans-Pareil, p 144

Cafés

Aux Quatre Jeudis, p 143
Byward Café, p 136
Café Quo Vadis, p 136
Clair de Lune, p 139
Country Corner Tea Room,
 p 146
Domus Café, p 140
Fou du Roi, p 144
Memories, p 136
Silk Road Café, p 137

Cajun

Cajun Attic, p 135

Canadian

National Arts Centre Café,
p 129

Chinese

Won Ton House, p 142
Yangtze, p 141

Creative

Echo Wine Café, p 130
Opus Bistro, p 142

Crepes

Café Crêpe de France,
p 137

Ethiopian

Addis Café, p 141

Fish and Seafood

Al's Steak and Seafood,
p 134
The Fish Market, p 139

French

Baccara, p 145
Café Henri Burger, p 145
Chez Jean-Pierre, p 133
Clair de Lune, p 139
Juniper, p 142
Le Métro, p 134
Le Panaché, p 144
Le Tartuffe, p 144

Hamburgers

Le Twist, p 144
Zak's Diner, p 137

Indian

Mukut, p 135
New Delhi, p 143
Shafali, p 137

Italian

Carmello, p 130
Fiori's, p 133
Fratelli, p 143
Mama Grazzy, p 138
Mangia, p 139
Piccolo Grande, p 137
Salvatore, p 141
Vittoria Trattoria, p 138

This chapter offers you a selection of a few good restaurants in the city. If you would like more information on Ottawa's restaurants, consult the *www.dine.net* web site.

The Rideau Canal

Ritz on the Canal
$$
375 Queen Elizabeth Dr.
at Fifth Ave.
☎*238-8998*
The menu at the Ritz on the Canal differs somewhat from those of its sister establishments in that it also features "gourmet" pizzas baked in a wood-burning oven. This restaurant is particularly appreciated in summer on account of its outstanding setting and huge terrace facing the canal at a point where it resembles a bay.

National Arts Centre Café
$$$
53 Elgin St.
☎*594-5127*
The Café of the National Arts Centre offers an un-

beatable view of the teeming activity on the Rideau Canal with boats in the summer and skaters in the winter. During the summer months, meals are served on a comfortable, well-designed terrace. Beyond a doubt, this is one of the most pleasant outdoor terraces in town, offering refined Canadian cooking. The chef makes inventive use of quality products from various regions of Canada. Grilled Atlantic salmon is a specialty. Not to be missed are the wonderful desserts. Prices are on the high side, however, unless a fixed-price menu is offered, which is rare.

Echo Wine Café
$$$-$$$$
221 Echo Dr.
☎234-1528
Those eager for new culinary experiences will be delighted with the Echo Wine Café. Day after day, the chef creates unique dishes blending unusual flavours, such as fillet of salmon with spicy *papadum* on a bed of curried rice enhanced with sweet apple sauce. Diners may be skeptical of the combinations offered, but will generally be delighted with the result. To better accompany each of the dishes, a selection of wines sold by the glass is available. The dishes are all delectable, but saving a little room for dessert is essential as these are equally innovative and mouthwatering.

Upper Town

Pancho Villa
$-$$
361 Elgin St.
☎234-8872
For a good but simple Mexican meal, the friendly Pancho Villa will not disappoint. Just next door is **Lois and Frimas**, whose excellent home-made ice creams are delectable.

The Colonnade
$-$$
280 Metcalfe St.
☎237-3179
If you love true American-style pizza with plenty of toppings, try The Colonnade which has had the market cornered for quite a while now. This spot is very simple and is divided into two sections; one of which is supposedly more chic than the other. The main attraction, however, is the pizza. All varieties come with cheese, but choosing the rest is up to you.

Carmello
$$
300 Sparks St.
On Sparks Street, a short distance from Parliament, you will find Carmello, a good restaurant to know in this neighbourhood. The

Ulysses's Favourites

For the best dining in Ottawa and Hull:
Clair de Lune, p 139
Domus Café, p 140
Le Métro, p 134
Le Sans-Pareil, p 144

For dessert:
Memories, p 136

For the elegant decor:
Wilfrid's, p 135
Friday's, p 133

For exotic cuisine:
Coriander Thai Cuisine, p 133

For the terrace:
Café du Centre National des Arts, p 129
Le Twist, p 144

establishment is most ap-pealing, with a dining room featuring large bay windows, a modern decor of wood and painted steel, and a delicious, simple menu where pasta and oven-baked pizza get top billing. And the portions are generous, too. Good quality for the price.

D'Arcy McGee
$$
44 Sparks St.
☎*230-4433*
If there is one place in Ottawa where you can enjoy a good meal in an unparalleled ambiance, it is definitely the D'Arcy McGee.

This typical Irish pub, located a stone's throw from Parliament Hill, is the haunt *par excellence* of the political staff. Friendly, convivial and frequented by a clientele of all ages, it has become one of the city's absolute musts.

The Mill Restaurant
$$$
555 Ottawa River Pkwy.
☎*237-1311*
Formerly, the banks of the Ottawa River were the industrial heart of the city. The Mill Restaurant is located in one of the few buildings from this area's past that has survived and been renovated. It now contains a vast, elegant dining room where guests

can savour house specialties that include steaks and roast beef. In summer, there is dining on the terrace as well. Without a doubt, this is one of the most enjoyable places to savour a meal in Ottawa.

Fairouz
$$
343 Somerset St. W.
☎233-1536
A little further west, the Fairouz restaurant occupies a beautiful, renovated Victorian house. If you like Lebanese specialties, go no further; the food here will delight you.

Johnny Farina
$$-$$$
216 Elgin St.
☎565-5155
In terms of decor, Johnny Farina has no cause to be envious of other very trendy restaurants on Elgin Street. Its vast dining room, graced with very high coffered ceilings, is adorned with a ceramic-tile floor, brick walls and a lovely black staircase. It is ideal for dining with friends, as you can have a good time and eat well without spending a fortune. The menu features dishes prepared with a modicum of originality such as tortellini with goat cheese sauce and pizzas baked in a wood- burning oven. Moreover, with the open kitchen looking directly onto the dining room you can watch the cooks in action while waiting for your meal. The only thing to find fault with here is the TV that's always on (though at low volume) in the corner.

Ritz
$$
274 Elgin St.
☎235-7027
Elgin Street is home to an institution known to just about everyone in town, the Ritz. Waiting is almost obligatory at this Italian restaurant which does not accept reservations. Its pasta dishes are deservedly renowned. Fortunately, this restaurant now has younger siblings. The **Ritz Uptown** *(226 Nepean, ☎238-8752)* is set in an old house, and reservations are accepted.

Connaught
$$-$$$
100 Elgin St.
☎234-6677
At the very end of the lobby of the Lord Elgin hotel, the Connaught is bathed in sunlight that pours in through its large glass veranda. The restaurant opens at the crack of dawn, so you can start the day with a good breakfast. The dinner menu features various dishes, including filet mignon and prime ribs.

Coriander Thai Cuisine

$$$

282 Kent St.

corner of Cooper St.

☎233-2828

The best Thai restaurant in town, Coriander Thai Cuisine is prized by fans of Asian food. A tiny, simply decorated place, where service is restrained, yet attentive, it fills up nightly with regulars who come to sample the many culinary wonders of the Kingdom of Siam. The menu features the region's classic specialties prepared by an uncompromising and supremely talented chef. The *satays* melt in your mouth, the lemon grass soup lets all its flavours shine through and both red and green curries are sheer delight.

Fiori's

$$$

239 Nepean St.

☎232-1377

Not far from the Ritz Uptown in another pretty little house is Fiori's, an Italian restaurant with excellent food. The veal dishes are especially delectable. The restaurant is small, friendly and full of charm. Service is warm and attentive. This comes at a price, of course, but it is worth it.

Chez Jean-Pierre

$$$

210 Somerset St. W.

☎235-9711

A little to the east toward Elgin Street, Chez Jean-Pierre does not have the most inviting of facades and the interior decor is not its strong point either. But these are things you can live with, for the fine French cuisine and the service are beyond reproach. This is a restaurant where quality is a long-time tradition.

Hy's Steak House

$$$

170 Queen St.

☎234-4545

≈234-1229

From its classic decor with dark-wood-panelled walls and muted ambiance, to the slightly stiff service, Hy's admirably upholds the steakhouse tradition. Carnivores are sure to appreciate the restaurant's appropriately tender, juicy steaks. There's a fine choice of salads as starters, some of which are prepared at your table.

Friday's

$$$

150 Elgin St.

☎237-5353

A feeling of well-being will sweep over you as soon as you walk into Friday's, which occupies a magnificent Victorian house built in 1875. With its large antique-decorated rooms, big wooden tables and high-backed chairs, which exude old-fashioned charm, the place is irresistible. Its rooms have been transformed into dining rooms where a relaxing atmosphere prevails. If the decor doesn't win you over, the succulent roast surely will. Of course, with all this going for it, Friday's has a devout following, so reservations are recommended.

Le Métro
$$$
315 Somerset St. W.
☎230-8123

Le Métro is undoubtedly one of the best eating spots in town. The *escargots* with roquefort in pastry are a true joy, as are the steak tartare or simple beef fillet with *béarnaise* sauce. The opulent, harmonious decor, the quiet atmosphere and the big, comfortable leather chairs assure you a relaxing and delicious evening.

Al's Steak and Seafood House
$$$-$$$$
327 Elgin St.
☎828-8349

Elgin Street features another choice place for real beef lovers: Al's Steak and Seafood House. This stylish restaurant has been delighting palates with perfectly tender and juicy prime beef for over 20 years now. Moreover, though the place's reputation was built on its toothsome steak, its seafood never disappoints.

Lower Town

Rideau Street

MarcheLino Mövenpick
$
Rideau St.
at Sussex Dr.
☎569-4934

Having a good meal in a shopping centre may seem illusory... And yet, MarcheLino Mövenpick, in the Rideau Centre, attracts crowds of happy diners. The restaurant's recipe for success is simple: a large dining-room, attractively decorated with plants and wooden tables, and delicious, quickly-prepared dishes from fresh, quality ingredients. In this lively place, everyone is free to stroll about and choose their dishes from one of the various stations where sushi, salads, pasta, quiches and all sorts of other dishes sure to please the most demanding palates are prepared before your eyes.

Good Morning Vietnam
$-$$
323 Rideau St.
☎789-4080

Heading east from the Rideau Centre, you will reach the Bytowne repertory cinema and its neighbour, Good Morning Vietnam. This little restaurant with its very plain decor lets the food do the talking, especially the hot and sour soup and the spring rolls.

Cajun Attic
$$
594 Rideau St.
☎789-1185

The delicacies of Louisiana cooking are yours to discover at the Cajun Attic, where each dish is more succulent than the last. You'll choose from favourites like chicken jambalaya or cajun curry with pecans. According to many this is the best cajun food in the city if not the region!

Mukut
$$
610 Rideau St.
☎789-2220

Hidden right at the end of the street, a short distance from the Rideau River, is Mukut, a very good Indian restaurant. Only the New Delhi on Bank Street can match the exquisite quality of the dishes prepared here. Located in an uninviting mini-mall, it lacks charm but the food is wonderful.

Santé
$$$
45 Rideau St.
☎241-7113

Located on the second floor of a building facing the Rideau Centre, Santé is easy to miss, so keep your eyes peeled. Its Californian, Thai and Caribbean specialties are true delights, especially the Bangkok noodles. This spot is an oasis of quiet repose with big bay windows opening onto some of the city's main attractions. Save room for something from the tempting dessert menu. Attentive service.

Wilfrid's
$$$-$$$$
1 Rideau St.
☎241-1414

Would a jaunt to the Château Laurier strike your fancy? If you go in for this kind of treat, head to Wilfrid's come lunch time (**$$**). You will thus be regaled with a warm dining room, comfortable armchairs, an unobstructed view of the Rideau Canal and a delicious but affordable lunch (prices of *à la carte* dishes are around $10). Coming here for breakfast is another pleasant little outing, but will cost you at least $10. On Sundays, however, it is best to opt for **Zoe's** for a delicious brunch (**$$$**) served in a quiet and elegant ambiance.

Around Byward Market

Since the Byward Market is the area most visited by tourists and locals alike, many restaurants have opened their doors here, some of which are definitely worth discovering. If you have sudden pangs of hunger or thirst, this is the place to be, especially in the summer. There are a number of friendly outdoor cafés and plenty of pedestrian traffic. In short, it is lively and very pleasant.

Beaver Tails
$
87 George St.
☎241-1230

Those with a sweet tooth will want to sample Beaver Tails, but don't be alarmed. These are merely delicious treats made from sugared deep-fried dough; something of a cross between a doughnut and a biscuit.

Byward Café
$
In the Byward Market

During the day, the Byward Market is full of life as crowds come here seeking out a treasure or two amidst its many stands. Here, you will also find the Byward Café, located in the market's main building. Shoppers can stop by for a cool beverage, a sandwich or a *panini*, served in a lovely dining room that overlooks the street's bustling activity.

Café Quo Vadis
$
Sussex Dr. at Clarence St.

Those craving a bite to eat after visiting one of the museums on Sussex Drive should stop by Café Quo Vadis, set up in a large,

rather cold space decorated with art work (which you can purchase). You will undoubtedly find something with which to appease your hunger here, for the place serves a good selection of cakes and coffees.

Earl of Sussex
$
431 Sussex Dr.
☎562-5544

The Earl of Sussex is a quintessential English pub: relaxed ambiance, woodwork, simple and nourishing fare and, above all, a wonderful selection of domestic and imported beers on tap. The place is hopping from noon to late afternoon.

Memories
$
7 Clarence St.
☎241-1882

Memories is almost always packed. Why? Because just about everyone in Ottawa comes to sample the many desserts that have made its reputation. The selection of cakes and pies of all sorts is so impressive that choosing can be a difficult task. But the greatest temptation may well be the delicious, oversized portions of apple pie. Light meals (interesting soups, sandwiches, salads) are also available. The delicious coffee makes a perfect accompaniment to whichever dessert you select.

Piccolo Grande
$
55 Murray
☎*241-2909*
For a *gelato* without equal,
Piccolo Grande is the place
to go, and the queues bear
witness to this. Here you
will find a large assortment
of exceptional quality
Italian ice cream, as well as
Neuhaus Belgian choco-
lates.

Zak's Diner
$
16 Byward Market
☎*241-2401*
Some spots draw attention
more for their decor than
for their food. This is the
case of Zak's Diner whose
bright lights and Coca-Cola
signs are meant to make it
look like a 1950s American
diner. The menu seems not
to have evolved since that
time, with the usual ham-
burgers, milk shakes and
fries served in large portions. This is a pleasant spot
for breakfast.

Blue Cactus
$-$$
2 Byward Market
☎*241-7061*
Blue Cactus is a Tex-Mex
restaurant with the usual
megacocktails, nachos (try
the very filling Blue Cactus
nachos), *fajitas* and so on.
The atmosphere at this
spot, which is popular with
young people, may be a
little too lively for some.

Café Shafali
$-$$
308 Dalhousie St.
☎*798-9188*
For reasonably priced In-
dian food, you might con-
sider Café Shafali, a small,
modest-looking restaurant
where you will enjoy no
less than excellent tandoori
dishes and perfectly fresh
nan bread.

Silk Road Café
$-$$
47 William St.
☎*241-4254*
If, by any chance, you are
looking for something a
little different, head to the
Silk Road Café which serves
Afghan food. This little restaurant's decor essentially
consists of salmon-pink and
black walls as well as a few
works of art for sale.
Though very simple, it has
a certain cachet. The lunch
menu features less exotic
dishes such as quiches,
chicken salads and burgers.

Café Crêpe de France
$$
76 Murray St.
☎*241-1220*
The Café Crêpe de France is
worth a visit for its Breton-
style crepes, its salads or for
its weekend brunch. The
setting is very agreeable,
with exposed brick, red-
and-white-checked table-
cloths, and subdued light-
ing. Big bay windows let in
plenty of daylight. In the
summer, you can opt for

the pretty little outdoor terrace. Besides crepes, different full-course meals are offered each day, but they aren't as good. This is an ideal spot for a light lunch or for a dessert crepe in the evening.

Casablanca
$$
41 Clarence St.
☎789-7855

If getting better acquainted with the flavours of Morrocco appeals to you, head to Casablanca, the restaurant. Their tasty dishes offer a wonderful opportunity to discover the flavours and aromas of this North-African region.

Mama Grazzy
$$
25 George St.
☎241-8656

Mama Grazzy unquestionably ranks among this area's most charming restaurants. It features two dining rooms: that on the main floor proves to be noisy and lively, while the one upstairs offers a quieter ambiance. But the pleasant outdoor terrace is definitely the best bet in summer. This is the place to go for original and delicious Italian specialties, which include a wide array of pasta dishes topped with one of four sauces. A variety of pizzas is also offered.

Ritz
$$
89 Clarence St.
☎789-9797

Those who are particularly fond of the cuisine at the Ritz restaurant will be pleased to know that a second one is located near the Byward Market.

Saigon Restaurant
$$
85 Clarence St.
in the Byward Market district
☎(613) 789-7934

In general, restaurants in the very touristy Byward Market area tend to be hard on the pocketbook; Saigon Restaurant is certainly an exception. It serves honest, authentic Vietnamese cooking at very reasonable prices in a typical Asian-restaurant setting. Apart from fixed-price meals, the menu features a vast array of dishes, including excellent and very filling soup meals in the tradition of Vietnamese cuisine.

Vittoria Trattoria
$$
35 William St.
☎789-8959

Vittoria Trattoria's pretty dining room with its stone walls and large windows opening out on the street offers an unparalleled cachet. There is also a second, large dining room upstairs, likewise graced with a stone wall; unfortunately, its ambiance is not as warm. Patrons will enjoy good Italian fare here.

Clair de Lune
$$-$$$
81B Clarence St.
☎ **241-2200**

Clair de Lune no longer needs an introduction in Ottawa. Indeed, for the past few years, it has been one of the most popular bistros in town, thanks to its classic French dishes and warm ambiance. The dining room's large bay windows allow diners to look out onto the lively street while savouring their meal. Those who prefer a more intimate spot will surely enjoy the back section of the dining

room. In addition, this restaurant offers an interesting wine list.

Mangia
$$-$$$
121 Clarence St.
☎ **562-4725**

What will undoubtedly catch your eye at the Mangia restaurant are the large picture windows, for the menu offers no surprises: pasta and good pizzas. Few would contest that this place is ideal for having a bite to eat on a sunny day. What's more, you don't have to spend a fortune.

The Fish Market
$$-$$$
54 York St.
☎ **241-3474**

Another institution in Ottawa is The Fish Market restaurant, set up on the approaches to the Byward Market and known throughout the capital since 1979. The dining room is decorated with nets, buoys and other objects related to fishing. That's only fit and proper in an establishment specializing in fish, shellfish and seafood, always served fresh. In addition, there are two other rooms on the first floor: **Coasters**, whose large picture windows look out on the bustling market, is just as congenial. Dishes here are less sophisticated (fish and chips) and more moderately priced, but quite good. The third room, **Vineyards**, is the place to go if all you want is a drink (good selection of wine by the glass) and a bite to eat. Shows are sometimes featured here.

Medithéo
$$-$$$

This restaurant with contemporary decor features colourful booths and modern art. Its hip clientele comes here to enjoy a varied menu, offering such dishes as omelets, Greek salads and fried calamari. There's something here to please every palate! In addition, a lovely terrace and large bay windows overlook the street.

🌴 Domus Café
$$$
85 Murray St.
☎ 241-6007

Domus Café is undoubtedly one of the best restaurants in Ottawa. The food is refined and innovative, made with the freshest of ingredients. Its success is derived from its original combinations of flavours. The menu changes every day but some of the most popular items keep reappearing. While choice is never exhaustive, the selection is interesting enough to make it difficult to decide. The desserts, limited to a choice of four or five, are of a calibre unequalled in Ottawa. The wine list includes excellent Californian wines, some of them available by the glass. And finally, try the Sunday brunch. It is divine and well worth the wait (reservations are not accepted for brunch).

Sandy Hill

🌴 Eclectic Noodle
$$$
287-B Somerset St. E.
corner of Russel St.
☎ 234-2428

A restaurant on the cutting edge of Ottawa's new wave, Eclectic Noodle is located slightly away from the action, in a residential area a few streets east of the University of Ottawa campus. This tiny restaurant with only a few tables features a simple setting with subtle lighting. Irresistible aromas wafting from the kitchens will set your mouth watering. Having mastered the preparation of all the succulently sauced pasta dishes that form the heart of the menu, the chef also creates poultry dishes. These include the surprising, delectable chicken with mango sauce and the Eclectic chicken—white meat stuffed with Brie, served with a mushroom and pine nut sauce. There are daily specials of appetizers and main dishes, which usually feature the irresistibly aromatic pastas.

Ottawa's Neighbourhoods

Heading west along Somerset Street West, you first come across **Chinatown**, between Bronson and Booth streets, which does not feature many truly outstanding restaurants, though the more popular ones always seem to be filled to capacity. **Little Italy** is next, along Preston Avenue and stretching south, and finally the **Wellington Street** area, which harbours plenty of good little eateries.

Chinatown

Rua Vang Golden Turtle
$
343 Booth St.
two streets south of Somerset St.
☎567-0074
Like every good Chinatown worthy of its name, Ottawa's small Chinese neighbourhood is packed with large and small restaurants of varying quality. The most expensive, though not necessarily the best, are found on Somerset Street, while the cross streets contain some small, cheap restaurants that are popular with neighbourhood regulars. Among these, one tiny place is outstanding because of unbeatable prices and the quality of its food. Rua Vang Golden Turtle, while unpretentious— with old-fashioned furniture in a plain setting—is renowned for its famous soup meals and its always delicious thin-noodle Vietnamese dishes. This place is so simple that customers write their own numerical orders on slips of paper that are then turned over to young servers whose role consists of delivering the dishes with a smile.

Yangtze
$$
700 Somerset St.
☎236-0555
Scores of restaurants with enticing menus succeed each other along Somerset Street in Chinatown. Yangtze ranks among those establishments with solid reputations. Indeed, the place is always full to capacity. Its prodigious dining room is equipped with large round tables and thus is ideal for Sunday family dinners. Though somewhat impersonal, it is nonetheless pleasant. The menu features delectable Cantonese specialties.

Little Italy

Salvatore
$$
388 Booth St.
☎233-4731
Also in Little Italy, Salvatore prepares good dishes in a quiet, gentle atmosphere without the excessive decor typical of some Italian restaurants.

Ottawa West

Addis Café
$$
closed Mon
1093 Wellington St.
☎725-5127
At the beginning of Wellington Street, in its least inviting and most forgotten part, lies hidden an exotic little pearl called Addis Café. This is a real discovery. Solomon, the friendly owner, will guide you cheerfully through the

wonders of Ethiopian cuisine, whose secret lies in combinations of different spices and seasonings. The setting is congenial: a small room with high ceilings and, on the walls, recent works of art that change every five or six weeks. The cooking will seduce you, especially if you like garlic, ginger and lentils. The basis of the menu is a flat, pancake-shaped bread called *injera* on top of which other food is served. Small portions of this bread are used to scoop up the puréed lentils or the long-simmering meat stews. Food can also be taken out. A must-taste!

Won Ton House
$$
1300 Wellington St.
☎ **728-8885**
Not far away, the Won Ton House is a neighbourhood favourite with Szechuanese and Cantonese dishes plus a few Indonesian items.

Juniper
$$-$$$
1293 Wellington St.
☎ **728-0220**
Another bistro, the Juniper opened its doors in this little-known area and soon left its mark. Consisting merely of small, coloured frames and parchment lamps, its sparse decor turns out to be both soothing and elegant. The two perfectly lovely dining

rooms are delightful. But what will catch your attention above all is the menu, featuring always toothsome and originally prepared dishes.

Opus Bistro
$$$$
closed Sun and Mon
1331 Wellington St.
☎ **722-9549**
Almost next door, Opus Bistro is worth the trip. With its dark, simple, tasteful decor, this small bistro serves tasty and impeccably presented dishes, some blending eclectic ingredients. Save room for the tempting desserts. The wine selection is enticing, by the glass or by the bottle. Service is outstanding and friendly with helpful advice on the best choices.

The Glebe

A number of boutiques with enticing window displays line Bank Street, near Glebe Street. These arrays are dazzling in the winter, especially in December, though you will have to dawdle along in order to truly contemplate them. Fortunately, you can then warm up and have something to eat at one of the pleasant **Starbucks**, **Guabbajabba** or **Second Cup** cafés located in the area. You will not be alone, however, for all three, with their selections of coffees and teas and mouthwatering goodies, are always full in the afternoons.

New Delhi
$$
683 Bank St.
☎ 237-4041

For excellent Indian dishes, make a reservation at the New Delhi. They offer dishes prepared with fresh quality ingredients, and the food is never too spicy. The chicken tikka, a tandoori specialty, is absolutely delicious. There is a buffet for under $10, every day except Saturday. It is also possible to order take-out items by telephone or at the counter.

Fratelli
$$-$$$
749 Bank St.
☎ 237-1658

Fratelli is one of those restaurants one chances upon with delight. The sober decor, essentially composed of splendid hardwood floors, wall lights and a few mirrors, makes the place inviting at first glance. The menu, is equally attractive, featuring Italian dishes tastefully prepared in an innovative way. A good place to keep in mind in the Glebe.

Hull

Aux Quatre Jeudis
$
44 Rue Laval
☎ 771-9557

An enjoyable café/restaurant/bar/gallery/movie theatre/terrace with a very laid-back atmosphere, Aux Quatre Jeudis is patronized by a young, slightly bohemian clientele. It shows movies and its pretty terrace is very popular in the summertime.

Pi-za'za
$
36 Rue Laval
☎ 771-0565

At Pi-za'za, you can sample an excellent variety of fine pizzas in a friendly, relaxed atmosphere.

Les Phoenix du Vietnam
$$
234 Montcalm, Hull
one street east of Blvd. Saint-Joseph
☎ (819) 771-2481

Les Phoenix du Vietnam has a very extensive menu. In a large dining room that isn't especially charming and is somewhat harshly lit, numerous, ever-loyal regulars savour the best of Vietnamese cuisine. If you ask a resident of Hull to name a restaurant with an excellent ratio of quality to price, one that's certain to please, the suggestion will probably be Les Phoenix du Vietnam. A good indication of quality!

Fou du Roi
$$
253 Boulevard Saint-Joseph
☎*778-0516*
The Fou du Roi serves simple, consistently good food. It's a popular lunch spot and has a attractive outdoor seating area during summer.

🍴 **Le Twist**
$$
88 Rue Montcalm
☎*777-8886*
Le Twist is known for its burgers, mussels and home-made fries, among the best in town, that are savoured in a charming setting and relaxed ambiance. In summer, a large, completely private terrace awaits you here. It is best to make reservations for lunch as the place is often jam-packed.

Le Panaché
$$$
closed Sun and Mon
201 Rue Eddy
☎*777-7771*
A little restaurant specializing in French cuisine, Le Panaché has a relaxed, intimate ambiance.

Le Pied Cochon
$$$
closed Sun and Mon
248 Rue Montcalm
☎*777-5808*
If you're looking for a good, unpretentious place to eat, head to Le Pied Cochon, where the food is as varied as it is delicious

and the service is impeccable.

La Soupière
$$$
closed Sun and Mon
53 Rue Kent
☎*771-6256*
A former private house, La Soupière offers excellent regional cuisine in large portions. As the restaurant is small, accommodating only 40 people, it is best to make reservations.

Le Tartuffe
$$$
closed Sun
133 Rue Notre Dame
☎*776-6424*
Le Tartuffe is a marvelous little gourmet French restaurant located just steps from the Musée Canadien des Civilisations. With its friendly, courteous service and delightful, intimate ambiance, this place is sure to win your heart.

🌴 **Le Sans-Pareil**
$$$-$$$$
closed Sun and Mon
71 Boulevard St-Raymond
☎*771-1471*
Le Sans-Pareil is located 5min from Hull's new casino, and right near the shopping centres. Since this is a Belgian restaurant, it's only normal that chef Luc Gielen offers a two-for-one special on mussels (prepared in twelve different ways) on Tuesday nights. The sinfully good menu

usually changes every three weeks, and focuses on fresh products from various parts of Québec. The chef has a flair for combining ingredients in innovative ways, so don't hesitate to opt for the *menu gourmand*. It includes several courses, complete with the appropriate wines to wash them down. This place may be small, but it's truly charming. Check it out!

The Casino has all the facilities for your gambling pleasure, and two restaurants which serve excellent meals away from all the betting. **Banco** *($$)* offers a reasonably priced, quality buffet and various menu items while the more chic and expensive **Baccara** *($$$$; closed for lunch; 1 Boulevard du Casino,* ☎772-6210) has won itself a place among the best restaurants of the region. The fixed-price menu always consists of superb dishes that you can enjoy along with spectacular views of the lake. The well-stocked wine cellar and impeccable service round out this memorable culinary experience.

The layout of the place definitely leaves something to be desired, however, as the noise from the gaming area seeps into the dining room. Diners are consequently continuously assailed with the din of slot machines, which disrupt the restaurant's muted ambiance. It is therefore best to request a table far from the entrance.

Café Henry Burger
$$$$
69 Rue Laurier
☎777-5646
The stylish Café Henry Burger specializes in fine French cuisine. The menu changes according to the availability of the freshest ingredients, and always offers dishes to please the most discerning palate. The restaurant has long maintained an excellent reputation.

Gatineau Park

Chelsea

 Soup'Herbe
$$
168 Chemin Old Chelsea, Chelsea
☎*(819) 827-7687*
A few minutes from L'Agaric, in a setting that is just as peaceful, Soup'Herbe's specialty is imaginative and refined vegetarian cuisine. This establishment, which is surrounded by trees, features a terrace that is greatly appreciated on hot summer days. In both kitchen and dining room, friendly, hospitable young staff make your meal as pleasant as possible. Aside from the

menu, the chef has a daily slate of suggested dishes. In summer, don't miss the delicious gaspacho. On weekends, brunch is available, including a main dish, salad, a delectable bun and a cinnamon roll.

L'Agaric
$$-$$$
254 Chemin Old Chelsea, Chelsea
☎*(819) 827-3030*
A cozy intimate restaurant in a quiet rural setting just a few minutes from the Gatineau Park, L'Agaric is set up in a charming little wooden house with an authentic country ambiance. The owner, of French origin, uses local produce to create culinary triumphs inspired by his native land. As appetizers, cream soups and delicious home-made pâtés are a good indication of what's to come—all just as delicious! To mention but two of the many fixed-price menus and *à la carte* dishes, the duck and lamb, both grilled, are sure winners—always tender and succulent.

Merrickville

Country Corner Tea room
$
Mill St.
The dining room of the Country Corner Tea room is very appealing with its an-

tique furniture and pretty wallpaper with little geese. Everything is in place in this haven of tranquillity. The menu offers simple, reasonably priced dishes, such as quiche.

Baldachin Restaurant
$$-$$$
111 St.Lawrence St.
☎*269-4223*
☎*877-881-8874*
⇋*469-4735*
Jakes Block, built in 1862, stands at the corner of Main and Lawrence and now houses the Baldachin Restaurant. Large picture windows look out onto the street and antique furniture give it the feeling of another era. The place is an absolute delight! The menu has several specialities that are always well prepared.

Sam Jakes Inn
$$$
118 Main St. E., K0G 1N0
☎*269-3711 or 800-567-4667*
⇋*269-3713*
www.samjakesinn.com
The restaurant of the Sam Jakes Inn features country-style furniture and pretty flowered wallpaper. The atmosphere is comfortable and the menu has a good selection of tasty and hearty dishes, though not the most innovative. The lamb chops, steak and trout all come with ample sauces and will satisfy any appetite.

Entertainment

Ottawa has never been famous for its nightlife.

Though its streets are often deserted after 11pm, you can top off your night enjoyably by knowing a few of its secrets. In addition to the warm pubs and lively bars, notably set up along Elgin Street and around Byward Market, the city has a flourishing cultural life. Excellent shows are presented at the National Arts Centre, where the city's various theatre companies perform. Finally, entertaining festivals are organized throughout the year.

Bars and Nightclubs

In the past, many Ontarians would finish off the night in Hull, because until very recently, only the bars in that city were open until 3am. Since April 1996, however, the two cities have adopted the same closing hours, so that bars in both Ottawa and Hull now close at 2am. Whatever your preference, you will find enjoyable bars on either side of the Ottawa River.

Near downtown Ottawa, there are several bars and pubs along Elgin Street, which is quite lively in the evening.

Ottawa

Maxwell's
340 Elgin St.
☎232-5771
Maxwell's, located above a restaurant, is popular with trendy youth. In the summer there's the advantage of a large balcony facing the lively street.

Lieutenant's Pump
361 Elgin St.
☎238-2949
Across the street is a very popular pub, Lieutenant's Pub. There are a few tables outside in the summer, and food is available.

Fox and Feather
283 Elgin St., at MacLaren St.
☎233-2219
If you are put off by flashy bars, you may appreciate the youthful and unpretentious atmosphere of the Fox and Feather. A bar and large picture windows are all that decorate this noisy, smoky room, but the ambiance here is quite appealing nonetheless.

Friday's Piano Bar
150 Elgin St.
☎237-5353
Friday's Piano Bar is more of a meeting spot for business people. It has an older clientele, some of whom end their evening here after

dining at the restaurant of the same name.

D'Arcy McGee
44 Sparks St.
The D'Arcy McGee pub can pride itself on being the only spot in Ottawa to bear the title of authentic Irish pub, for the interior was completely built in Ireland, then transported to Ottawa where it was reconstructed piece by piece. Fitted with woodwork and stained-glass windows and decorated with scores of marvellous knick-knacks, this warm and inviting bar is always full. Concerts are presented here on certain evenings. Good selection of beers on tap.

Yuk Yuk's Comedy Cabaret
Wed to Sat
88 Albert St.
☎236-5233
Yuk Yuk's is part of a chain offering comedy shows, some of them actually quite funny. This is an interesting alternative to a conventional bar.

The Manx
370 Elgin St. (downstairs at the corner of Elgin and Frank)
☎231-2070
Small and smoky, this pub is a popular spot with artists, literary types and the city's contingent of media professionals. Maybe it's the

menu, featuring more than the usual pub fare, made fresh and from scratch; or possibly it's the 16 micro-brewery drafts on-tap; but it is probably the formidable selection of single malt scotch (50 at last count) that draws a loyal crowd. If the libations aren't to your taste, go for brunch, but go early—it's full by 10:30am.

The Mercury Lounge
56 ByWard Market (upstairs)
☎789-5324
www.mercurylounge.net
A two-storey swoop of red velvet drape adds to the stylish ambience at the Mercury Lounge, which caters to the 25 and up crowd. The music is eclectic: re-examined jazz, Afro, funk, soul, modern, Brazilian and worldbeat. The art changes monthly with exhibitions of challenging regional artists. The martinis are creative and the feeling is both dynamic and smooth.

The area around the Byward Market is home to several bars, many of them clustered along George and York streets.

Stoney's
62 York St.
☎241-8858
Stoney's probably holds the record of longevity for clubs. It seems young people have been coming here forever to have a drink and cut loose on the small dance floor. In the summer, another section is open in back. The music generally tends towards rock and roll.

Vineyard's Wine Bar Bistro
54 York St.
☎241-4270
Vineyard's Wine Bar Bistro is a friendly, congenial little bar where you can enjoy wine, beer and cheese. Musicians often perform here, with jazz at the top of the list.

Atomic
137 Besserer St.
☎241-2411
With little more than a mail-box and steel door marking its location, Atomic is its own best advertisement; club enthusiasts from as far away as New York City line up around the block for full, glorious immersion in sound and light. Atomic features both international and resident DJ talent, simultaneously combining two floors of music, drink and communal ambiance. Pick a floor, or let gravity make the decision for you. After losing yourself in the sound and movement, it is not uncommon to leave Atomic while the rest of the world is waking up for work.

The Laff
42 York St.
☎241-4747

This Ottawa institution has been in operation for over 150 years and bills itself as the city's oldest tavern. Apparently everyone in Ottawa has been to the Laff at one time or another and the crowd is diverse. The recently updated menu does include vegetarian choices. The Laff is an informal and historical stop after an afternoon in the ByWard Market.

Hard Rock Café
73 York St.

Part of the well-known chain, Ottawa's Hard Rock Café is a carbon copy of its sister establishments. It is decked out with banquettes and electric guitars on the walls.

Heart and Crown
67 Clarence St.
☎562-0674

Though lacking the character of the D'Arcy McGee, the Heart and Crown is another fashionable Irish pub in the capital. Relaxed ambiance and good selection of beers.

Earl of Sussex
431 Sussex Dr.
☎532-5544

Ottawa just wouldn't be right without an English pub: so the Earl of Sussex was thus set up here. Its warm decor, beer on tap and menu featuring fish and chips are entirely befitting of this type of establishment.

Market Station Bar Bistro
15 George St. (enter at the side)
☎562-3540

The terrace at the Market Station is one of the best in the city, situated in a courtyard framed by heritage buildings in the ByWard Market and offering a shaded area for the hottest summer afternoons. This gay and lesbian bistro also offers live entertainment that makes for traffic-stopping window dressing every Friday night.

Zoe's
1 Rideau St.

If the mere thought of spending hours in a smoky space where a mixed crowd jigs to the sounds of deafening music makes you shudder, opt for the chic Zoe's at the Château Laurier. Everything here is calm and comfy; the place boasts delightfully soft music and cosy armchairs.

Hull

Aux Quatre Jeudis
44 Laval

For many years now, Aux Quatre Jeudis has been *the* place for the café crowd. It has lots of ambiance, and in the summer its big, attractive terrace is a great place to hang out.

Le Bop
5 Aubry

This is a pleasant little place in old Hull. You can kick off your evening with a reasonably priced, decent meal. The music ranges from techno and disco to soft rock and even a little hard rock.

Le Fou du Roi
253 Boulevard St-Joseph

Le Fou du Roi is where the thirty-something crowd hangs out. There's a dance floor, and the windows open onto a little terrace in the summertime. This place is also a popular after-work gathering place.

Theatres

National Arts Centre
53 Elgin St.
☎996-5051
⇌996-9578

The National Arts Centre is Ottawa's cultural headquar-ters, with an opera house and two theatres where top-notch performances are offered year-round.

Ottawa has several theatre companies in addition to those staging their plays at the National Arts Centre.

Great Canadian Theatre Company
910 Gladstone Ave.
☎236-5196

The Great Canadian Theatre Company presents plays by Canadian dramaturges.

Ottawa Little Theatre
400 King Edward Ave.
☎233-8948

The Ottawa Little Theatre is a community theatre company that often stages interesting plays.

Odyssey Theatre
$18
2 Daly Ave.
☎232-8407

The Odyssey Theatre is distinctive in that it specializes in outdoor plays. During the summer, the company performs in Strathcona Park.

Movie Theatres

Cineplex Odeon
World Exchange Plaza
111 Albert St.

386 Somerset W.

Entertainment

Famous Players
Capital Square
230 Queen St.

Rideau Centre
50 Rideau St.

Bytowne
325 Rideau St.
(repertory cinema)

Casino

Casino de Hull
11pm to 3am
1 Boulevard du Casino
☎*(819) 772-2100*
☎*800-665-2274*
Those looking to have fun while standing a good chance of winning a fair amount of money can head to the Casino de Hull. The vast casino notably comprises slot machines, Keno, blackjack and roulette tables, as well as two restaurants (see p 145).

Festivals and Cultural Events

February

Winterlude no longer needs an introduction: its reputation is well established in Canada. For the first three weekends in February winter festivities of all sorts are held, during which it is possible to participate in myriad sports events.

May

The **Tulip Festival** is held for approximately 10 days in May. The city is then decked with thousands of tulips, bestowed by the Netherlands as a show of thanks to Canada for taking in Queen Wilhemina during the Second World War. Shows and activities of all kinds in various parts of the city, including Confederation and Major's Hill parks.

June

The **Festival Franco-Ontarien** is held at the end of June. This is a celebration of French culture in Ontario. There are activities of all sorts, handicrafts stalls, and an important series of shows presenting many of the greats of French song from here and elsewhere.

Another major event in the capital, the **Super Francofête**, which celebrates French culture, will be held from June 24 to July 24, 2001 (☎749-5389, *www.jeux2001.ca)*. Participants from 52 Francophone countries will attend to be part of the festivities. This

Les Jeux de la Francophonie Games

In July 2001, Ottawa and Hull will host the 5th Jeux de la Francophonie games, which are held every four years and welcome both athletes from all sports disciplines, and artists from various cultural fields. The goal of these games is to bring French-speaking countries closer together and to promote francophone culture.

During the games, countless sports and cultural activities will be featured at different venues in the two cities. Street shows and music, story-telling and poetry contests are some of the events that will highlight the importance of francophone culture throughout the world. Sporting competitions, such as basketball, soccer, track and field, and beach volleyball, will also be held.

event will also feature a number of sports and cultural events.

July

Canada Day is celebrated on July 1. This is a day when countless activities are organized, such as outdoor shows featuring some of the greatest Canadian artists.

In early July, the blues take over as the nation's capital welcomes a few of the biggest names in blues for the three days of the **Ottawa Citizen Bluefest** (☎233-8798). Concerts take place at Confederation Park.

In the last two weeks of July, jazz enthusiasts get their turn to enjoy themselves while the **Ottawa International Jazz Festival**

Entertainment

(☎594-3580,
www.jazz.ottawa.com) is in
full swing. Concerts at Confederation Park.

In late July, aficionados of
chamber music won't want
to miss the **Ottawa Chamber
Music Festival** (☎234-8008),
during which many con-
certs are presented in the
city's churches.

During **Gay Pride** week, in
mid-July, a host of activities
(parade, picnic and shows)
take place in order to cele-
brate the city's gay and
lesbian community.

Casino

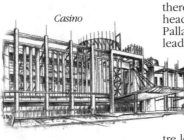

August

The casino's opening was
the origin of an annual
fireworks festival, **Les Grands
Feux du Casino**
(☎819-771-FEUX or
800-771-FEUX), held every
year during the month of
August.

Spectator Sports

Ottawa has had its own
National Hockey League
(NHL) team, the **Senators**
(*1000 Palladium Dr.,*
☎771-7367 or 800-444-7367,
≈599-0358,
www.ottawasenators.com),
since 1992. Those who wish
to attend one of the games
played at the Corel Centre
must head to Kanata, which
is located a dozen kilo-
metres from town. To get
there by car, take the 417
heading west and turn off at
Palladium Drive, which
leads straight to the arena.
If you prefer public
transportation, take
a bus at one of the
Transitway stations,
then transfer to
one of the stops
with the Corel Cen-
tre logo (buses 401, 402,
403, 404 and 405 all stop at
the centre).

The **Ottawa Lynx** (*300 Coven-
try Rd.,* ☎747-5969 or
800-663-0985, ≈747-0003,
www.magi.com/lynx/), the
local baseball team, is a
subsidiary of the National
Baseball League's Montreal
Expos. Those attending the
games played by the Lynx
will be treated to a match of
excellent calibre as this is
the ultimate grade before
the major leagues.

Shopping

Ottawa has plenty to offer those who consider shopping along main thoroughfares bordered by enticing shop windows among the pleasures of travelling.

Indeed, the city features four areas that are ideal for abandoning yourself entirely to shopping: Sparks Street, Bank Street, Elgin Street and the area surrounding Byward Market. Year-round, each area displays its own particular charm. In summer, Byward Market, with its flower, fruit and vegetable vendors, is unquestionably the liveliest. During the holiday season, the area around Bank Street has a unique cachet as the city is festooned with an abundance of lights. One thing is sure, whatever the time of year, you will be able to unearth a thousand and one finds as you discover the streets of the capital.

Upper Town

Sparks Street, a long pedestrian-only thoroughfare lined with trees, benches and lovely shops, makes for a very pleasant little stroll. On rainy days, when walking the streets proves less appealing, try the **240 Sparks** shopping centre, which comprises several attractive boutiques. Among these is **Holt Renfrew**, which offers a wide choice of high-quality items, including men's and women's clothing designed by great European, American and Canadian designers, plus beauty products and accessories.

Kitchen Supplies

McIntosh & Watts
193 Sparks St.
☎*236-9644*
You'll need to proceed with care upon entering the rather cluttered McIntosh & Watts boutique, where crystal vases and glasses, china, candelabras and knick- knacks of all kinds vie for space in a somewhat precarious fashion. Caution is all the more necessary as some of these exquisite items are quite expensive. You will not fail, however, to unearth something here that's sure to beautify your home.

Handicrafts

Snow Goose
83 Sparks St.
☎*232-2213*
Sparks Street, between Elgin and O'Connor streets, is a good place to shop for Canadian-made handicrafts. The first among many such shops is the Snow Goose, which boasts a wide selection of creations by Inuit and First Nations artisans, including sculptures and engravings. The shop also carries an abundance of leather and fur accouterments, such as mocassins, gloves and hats.

Canada's Four Corners
93 Sparks St.
☎*233-2322*
A stone's throw away, Canada's Four Corners also sells Native-American handicrafts; however, finding a good-quality item requires rummaging and sorting through the assorted junk and plastic objects. Plastic place mats, T-shirts bearing Canada's colours, Inuit sculptures and leather mocassins are all jumbled together here. At the very back of the store are reproductions of engravings by native artists (Norval Morisseau, Benjamin Chee-Chee, Doris Cyrette, etc.), perhaps the greatest find in the place.

Office Supplies

Grand & Toy
116 Albert St.
☎*233-6718*
This is hardly a place worth rushing to, but it is a useful address if you are looking for envelopes, paper, notebooks, pencils, or any office supplies you may be short

of during your stay.

Books

Place Bell Books
175 Metcalfe St.
☎*233-3821*
This store offers books on numerous different subjects, as well as a good selection of travel guides.

Smithbooks
240 Sparks St.
☎*233-5901*
You can also check out the incredible selection at the Smithbooks shop. In addition to a wide choice of works about Canada, the place carries books dealing with various subjects, as well as novels, beautiful tomes and travel guidebooks.

Maison de la Presse Internationale
92 Bank St.
☎*230-9774*
For magazines and newspapers, head to Maison de la Presse Internationale.

Stamps and Antique Prints

Ian Kimmerly Stamps
112 Sparks St.
☎*235-9119*
Upon entering the small, cluttered Ian Kimmerly Stamps shop, you will feel as if you've gone back in time, for antique prints, often over 100 years old, take up every inch of space. The place also has a small section devoted to stamps, which is mainly patronized by collectors who come to spend hours indulging their passion: searching through mountains of little stamps for the most valuable one.

Lower Town

Rideau Centre
50 Rideau St.
☎*236-6565*
A shopping mall *par excellence* in the capital, the Rideau Centre, with some 200 shops, is unquestionably the place to find anything and everything. Noteworthy among this succession of stores of all kinds are HMV (music store), the Disney store, Oh Yes Ottawa (for souvenirs of the city), Mrs. Tiggy Winkles (toys), The Gap (clothing for all) and Roots (leather garments). The centre also houses two pharmacies, banks (Royal, Nova Scotia, TD), as well as several fast-food restaurants and Marché Mövenpick (see p 134).

For window shopping and some interesting finds, nothing beats a stroll around the **Byward Market**. Winter or summer, the central pavilion, where vegetable dealers gather in the

Shopping

summer, houses a multitude of handicraft stalls on two floors. You can buy all sorts of items: jewellery, leather goods, scarves, paintings, and so on. The vegetable market lies at the heart of the action in the summer. It is a pleasant spot to shop or merely to linger.

Kitchen Supplies

Domus Housewares
85 Murray St.
☎241-6410
Domus is not only the name of a very good restaurant (see p 140), but also the name of a top-of-the-line kitchenware store. Domus Housewares is vast and bright. Besides selling almost every kitchen accessory imaginable, it offers cookbooks for every taste.

Sporting Goods

Mountain Equipment Co-op
366 Richmond Rd., Roxborough
☎729-2700
Backpacks, top-quality camping material at good prices, and sports clothes are part of the assortment you will find at MEC. This is the place to go to equip yourself for an outdoor excursion.

Jewellery

Striking
531A Sussex Dr.
☎562-9398
Those who appreciate unusual jewels should drop by Striking, whose gold or silver earrings, necklaces, brooches and bracelets are sure to prove irresistible.

Home Decoration

Côte Sud
Sussex Dr.
Whether you are looking for lamps, candelabras, mirrors, dishes or furniture, dropping by Côte Sud is sure to give you lots of original ideas for beautifying your home. Indeed, the hardest thing about visiting this shop will be resisting its many temptations.

Zone
471 Sussex Dr.
If you have left Côte Sud unscathed or, rather less likely, without having found exactly what you wanted, head to the Zone boutique, located a short distance away, which offers an equally enticing selection of interior decor objects.

Folio
459 Sussex Dr.
☎241-6336
Folio is another good place for home decorations, particularly for those ready

to make extravagant pur-
chases such as a Kosta
Boda vase or an Alesi item.

Christmas & Candles
481 Sussex Dr.
☎241-5476
Those who consider buying
Christmas decorations in the
middle of July to be per-
fectly normal will be de-
lighted with the Christmas
& Candles shop, which
overflows with tree decorations and ornaments of all
kinds year-round.

Food

Bagel Bagel
92 Clarence St.
☎241-8998
This is an establishment that
prepares bagels in 1,001
ways. The countless varieties of bagels produced here
are sold at the counter.
Something for every taste.

Valley Goods Company
41 York St.
☎241-3000
Close by, the Valley Goods
Company offers various
products in the tradition of
an old-fashioned general
store. You can buy choco-
late, jams, chutneys, ice
cream, original greeting
cards, and an array of other
items.

Gift Ideas

National Gallery of Canada
380 Sussex Dr.
The museum shop at the
National Gallery of Canada
is just the place for those
who like to rummage for
hours through a
mind-boggling amount of
reproductions, be they
posters, jewellery or decorative objects. In addition to
these quality copies, the
boutique contains an amaz-
ing collection of art books
as well as works by Na-
tive-American and Canadian
artisans and sculptors.

Planet BD
493 Sussex Dr.
☎789-6307
Fans of Tintin or Asterix
should head to Planet BD,
where several figurines and
effigies of these comic-book
heroes are displayed. The
cost of some of these items
may seem exorbitant, but,
after having admired the
finely detailed hand-made
objects, you will consider
them as small works of art
rather than mere parapher-
nalia.

Cow's
43 Clarence St.
☎244-4224
Finding the appropriate
words to describe Cow's
can prove rather difficult.
The shop notably carries
T-shirts and other cotton
apparel, coffee mugs and

various kitchen items, all adorned with stylized cows and short, amusing captions. Delicious ice-cream is also served here.

Books, Newspapers and Magazines

Chapters
Rideau St., at Sussex Dr.
Part of the huge chain of bookshops, Ottawa's Chapters offers an incredible selection of books for all tastes, in both English and French.

Librairie du Soleil
321 Dalhousie St.
☎ *241-6999*
There is really only one place to procure French books in the nation's capital: Librairie du Soleil.

Right beside the Byward Market **Globes** sells both local and foreign newspapers and magazines.

Desmarais Robitaille
333 Dalhousie St.
☎ *241-1175*
A few steps away is the Desmarais Robitaille shop, which specializes in religious books and objects.

World of Maps and Travel
1235 Wellington St.
☎ *724-6776*
Those who want to stock up on travel guides and road maps will have to leave the downtown area to get to World of Maps and Travel, which is basically the only shop specialized in this field in the Ottawa region.

Coins

Royal Canadian Mint
320 Sussex Dr.
Numismatists should not fail to visit the shop at the Royal Canadian Mint, in the very building where collectable Canadian coins are minted. The very latest creations, in silver, gold and platinum, are displayed here for sale.

Stationery

The Papery
11A William St.
☎ *241-1212*
The Papery is the perfect place to find stationery, such as beautiful greeting cards, agendas, calendars, wrapping paper and storage boxes of all sizes.

Beauty Products

Belle de Provence
Georges St., at Dalhousie St.
The displays are so lovely and the products smell so good at the Belle de Provence boutique, you may well have the uncontrollable urge to buy everything in sight. Mild soaps for

softer skin, natural shampoos... enough to make you indulge in a spending spree!

The Glebe

In fine weather, you may leave Sparks Street and explore Bank Street, another one of Ottawa's pleasant main thoroughfares. As you walk along, the street becomes alternately dull and seductive, but it will not fail to charm you. It is home to two distinct commercial sections: one around Somerset Street and a second one south of Queensway.

Kitchen Supplies

Great Glebe Emporium
724 Bank St.
☎233-3474
No one should purchase any kitchen article whatsoever without having first compared its price at the Great Glebe Emporium. The shelves here are jam-packed with plates, glasses, bowls, saucepans (notably Paderno brand) and frying pans, always sold at discount prices. In places, extricating the coveted item from the shelf without knocking anything down can seem a daunting task. Another piece of advice before entering: summon up your patience, for the aisles are

narrow and the shop is always crowded.

J. D. Adam
795 Bank St.
☎235-8714
Right next door, J. D. Adam harbours fewer low-priced treasures, but still contains a good selection of quality items as well as various decorative objects.

Home Decoration

East Wind
794 Bank St.
☎567-0382
The Orient has always inspired dreaming. By popping over to the East Wind boutique, you may succeed in finding some treasure that evokes these distant lands.

Toys

Mrs. Tiggy Winkles
809 Bank St.
☎234-3836
The very beautiful high-quality toys at Mrs. Tiggy Winkles have been delighting children since time immemorial.

Art Supplies

Paintbrushes, pencils, sketch pads... Two good places to know about in the capital are **Wallack's** (231 Bank St., ☎234-1800) and

Shopping

Omer Deserres, also on Bank Street.

Stationery

The Papery
850 Bank St.
☎*230-1313*
You will find another outlet of The Papery in the Glebe shopping area which also features lovely stationery (pens, greeting cards, wrapping paper, etc.), just like its sister shop near the Byward Market.

Clothing

La Cache
763 Bank St.
☎*233-0412*
At La Cache, you are sure to find a little something which pleases you, for the boutique overflows with a profusion of goods: cotton and wool garments, scarves and hats of all kinds, beauty products, bedding, knick-knacks and dishes.

Roots
787 Bank St.
For leather bags, shoes and coats, both casual and durable, head to Roots, whose reputation is long-standing. Other items, such as wool sweaters, are also worth the trip.

Penelope's Haberdashery
81 Bank St.
☎*232-9565*
Piles and piles and sweaters in every colour of the rainbow clutter the walls of Penelope's Haberdashery. Finding something here therefore entails taking the time to rummage through the countless, often classically cut, but always high-quality wool sweaters.

Hull

Canadien Museum of Civilization
100 Rue Laurier
The boutique of the Canadian Museum of Civilization is, in a way, part of the exhibit. Although the Canadian and Aboriginal craft pieces aren't of the same quality as those exhibited at the museum, you'll find all sorts of reasonably priced treasures and lots of great little curios.

The museum also has a **bookstore** with a wonderful collection on the history of crafts in many different cultures.

Place Cartier
425 St. Joseph Blvd.
☎*(819) 777-2133*
Outside the downtown area is the Place Cartier shopping centre. Among its many shops, the **Librairie du Soleil** (☎*819-595-2414*) is a great place for those who

might be interested in purchasing books in French.

Les Galeries de Hull
320 St. Joseph Blvd.
☎*(819) 770-7925*
Not too far from Place Cartier is a second shopping centre, Les Galeries de Hull. **Librairie Réflexion** *(☎819-776-4919)* offers books of all kinds as well as magazines and stationery. A small post office is also located here.

Merrickville

Mirick's Landing
St. Lawrence St.
Mirick's Landing sells a fine variety of items, including soaps, candles, tablecloths and napkins, and various trinkets.

Index

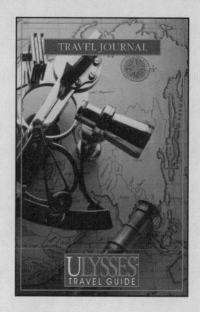

Travel Notes

El placer de viajar mejor

e plaisir de mieux voyager

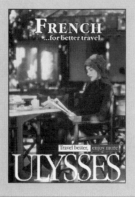

Order Form

Ulysses Travel Guides

☐ Acapulco ..... $14.95 CAN / $9.95 US	☐ Lisbon .... $18.95 CAN / $13.95 US
☐ Atlantic Canada $24.95 CAN / $17.95 US	☐ Louisiana ..... $29.95 CAN / $21.95 US
☐ Bahamas ..... $24.95 CAN / $17.95 US	☐ Martinique .... $24.95 CAN / $17.95 US
☐ Beaches of Maine $12.95 CAN / $9.95 US	☐ Montréal ..... $19.95 CAN / $14.95 US
☐ Bed & Breakfasts $14.95 CAN / in Québec $10.95 US	☐ Miami .... $9.95 CAN / $12.95 US
☐ Belize .... $16.95 CAN / $12.95 US	☐ New Orleans .. $17.95 CAN / $12.95 US
☐ Calgary ...... $17.95 CAN / $12.95 US	☐ New York City . $19.95 CAN / $14.95 US
☐ Canada .... $29.95 CAN / $21.95 US	☐ Nicaragua ..... $24.95 CAN / $16.95 US
☐ Chicago ...... $19.95 CAN / $14.95 US	☐ Ontario ...... $27.95 CAN / $19.95US
☐ Chile .... $27.95 CAN / $17.95 US	☐ Ontario's Best Hotels and Restaurants ... $27.95 CAN / $19.95US
☐ Colombia ..... $29.95 CAN / $21.95 US	☐ Ottawa .... $17.95 CAN / $12.95 US
☐ Costa Rica .... $27.95 CAN / $19.95 US	☐ Panamá ...... $24.95 CAN / $17.95 US
☐ Cuba .... $24.95 CAN / $17.95 US	☐ Peru .... $27.95 CAN / $19.95 US
☐ Dominican .... $24.95 CAN / Republic $17.95 US	☐ Phoenix ...... $16.95 CAN / $12.95 US
☐ Ecuador and .. $24.95 CAN / Galápagos Islands $17.95 US	☐ Portugal ...... $24.95 CAN / $16.95 US
☐ El Salvador .... $22.95 CAN / $14.95 US	☐ Provence - .... $29.95 CAN / Côte d'Azur $21.95US
☐ Guadeloupe ... $24.95 CAN / $17.95 US	☐ Puerto Rico ... $24.95 CAN / $17.95 US
☐ Guatemala .... $24.95 CAN / $17.95 US	☐ Québec .... $29.95 CAN / $21.95 US
☐ Hawaii .... $29.95 CAN / $21.95 US	☐ Québec City ... $17.95 CAN / $12.95 US
☐ Honduras ..... $24.95 CAN / $17.95 US	☐ Québec and Ontario with Via .... $9.95 CAN / $7.95 US
☐ Islands of the .. $24.95 CAN / Bahamas $17.95 US	
☐ Las Vegas ..... $17.95 CAN / $12.95 US	

☐ Seattle .... $17.95 CAN	☐ Vancouver .... $17.95 CAN
$12.95 US	$12.95 US
☐ Toronto ...... $18.95 CAN	☐ Washington D.C. $18.95 CAN
$13.95 US	$13.95 US
☐ Tunisia .... $27.95 CAN	☐ Western Canada $29.95 CAN
$19.95 US	$21.95 US

Ulysses Due South

☐ Acapulco ..... $14.95 CAN	☐ Los Cabos .... $14.95 CAN
$9.95 US	and La Paz $10.95 US
☐ Belize .... $16.95 CAN	☐ Puerto Plata - . $14.95 CAN
$12.95 US	Sosua $9.95 US
☐ Cancún & ..... $19.95 CAN	☐ Puerto Vallarta . $14.95 CAN
Riviera Maya $14.95 US	$9.95 US
☐ Cartagena .... $12.95 CAN	☐ St. Martin ..... $16.95 CAN
(Colombia) $9.95 US	and St. Barts $12.95 US
☐ Huatulco - .... $17.95 CAN	
Puerto Escondido $12.95 US	

Ulysses Travel Journals

☐ Ulysses Travel Journal	☐ Ulysses Travel Journal
(Blue, Red, Green, Yellow,	(80 Days) ..... $14.95 CAN
Sextant) .... $9.95 CAN	$9.95 US
$7.95 US	

Ulysses Green Escapes

☐ Cycling in France $22.95 CAN	☐ Hiking in the .. $19.95 CAN
$16.95 US	Northeastern U.S. $13.95 US
☐ Cycling in ..... $22.95 CAN	☐ Hiking in ..... $19.95 CAN
Ontario $16.95 US	Québec $13.95 US

Title	Qty	Price	Total

Name:	Subtotal	
	Shipping	$4 CAN $3 US
Address:	Subtotal	
	GST in Canada 7%	
	Total	

Tel: Fax:

E-mail:

Payment: ☐ Cheque ☐ Visa ☐ MasterCard

Card number_____

Expiry date_____

Signature_____

ULYSSES TRAVEL GUIDES

4176 St-Denis,
Montréal, Québec,
H2W 2M5
☎(514) 843-9447
fax (514) 843-9448

305 Madison Avenue,
Suite 1166,
New York, NY 10165

Toll-free: 1-877-542-7247
Info@ulysses.ca
www.ulyssesguides.com